MOUNTAIN BIKE MAINTENANCE

HOW TO MAINTAIN AND REPAIR YOUR MOUNTAIN BIKE

ROB VAN DER PLAS

CYCLE PUBLISHING / VAN DER PLAS PUBLICATIONS, SAN FRANCISCO

Printed in Hong Kong

Publisher's information:
Cycle Publishing / Van der Plas Publications
1282 7th Avenue
San Francisco, CA 94122
USA
http://www.cyclepublishing.com
E-mail: con.tact@cyclepublishing.com

Distributed or represented to the book trade by:
USA: Midpoint Trade Books, Kansas City, KS
UK: Orca Book Services / Chris Lloyd Sales & Marketing Services, Poole, Dorset
Australia: Tower Books, Frenchs Forest, NSW
Canada: Accent Technical Publications, Cambridge, ON

Cover design:
Kent Lytle, Lytle Design, Alameda, CA

Photography:
Neil van der Plas, San Rafael, CA

With special thanks to American Cyclery in San Francisco for providing equipment used for
some of the text and cover photos

Publisher's Cataloging in Publication Data
Van der Plas, Rob. Mountain Bike Maintenance: How to repair and maintain your mountain
bike
1. Bicycles and bicycling—handbooks and manuals
23 cm. 176 p. Bibliography. Includes index
I. Title: How to maintain and repair your mountain bike
II. Authorship
Library of Congress Control Number: 2006932243
ISBN 1-892495-53-8 / 978-1-892495-53-2

TABLE OF CONTENTS

INTRODUCTION

The modern mountain bike has come a long way. It has gone through a short but turbulent development over the quarter century since its introduction, and is now at a stage of mature development. However, things do wear out, they do come loose, they do get out of adjustment, and sometimes they break.

That's why any bicycle needs maintenance and repair work. Maintenance is the work done to prevent any potential problems as much as possible before they occur, while repair is what's done to fix things if they do break down. This book covers both, but the emphasis is on preventive maintenance, because on today's mountain bike, many of the components, such as suspension and disk brakes, are essentially closed systems that can't be "fixed" by the home mechanic, so you will be better off referring those to a bicycle mechanic.

Chapters 1 and 2 deal with general maintenance issues, while the remaining chapters of the book each covers a spe-cific functional group of components and its maintenance.

A warning about terminology used in this book: not everybody calls the various parts of the bike, and the various tools used, by the same names. What's called a wrench in the U.S. is called a spanner or a key (depending on just what kind of wrench is meant) in Britain. This book adheres primarily to the terminology and spelling conventions common in the U.S., giving alternate terminology in parentheses only where it might otherwise not be clear what is meant.

Although I have tried to offer step-by-step instructions wherever appropriate, you will have to look out for peculiarities of the bike you're working on. Despite the many things all bikes and their components have in common, they're not all identical, even within the same bicycle type. Consequently, you will have to make whatever adaptations it takes to apply the general instructions to your specific situation.

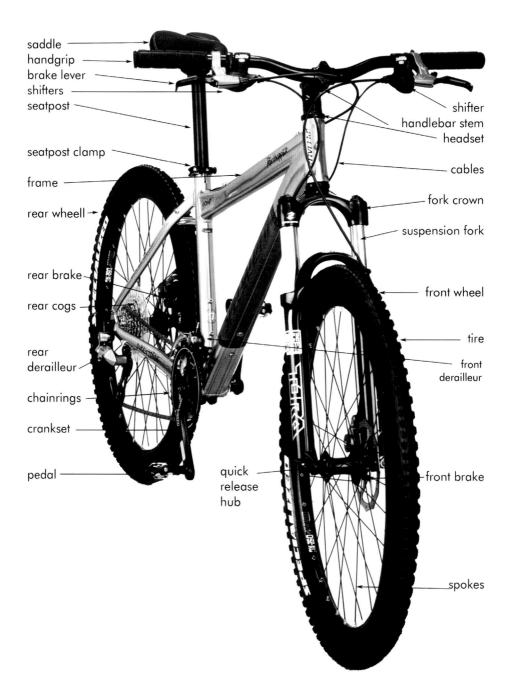

saddle
handgrip
brake lever
shifters
seatpost

shifter
handlebar stem
headset

seatpost clamp

cables

frame

fork crown

rear wheell

suspension fork

rear brake

front wheel

rear cogs

tire

rear
derailleur

front
derailleur

chainrings

crankset

pedal

quick
release
hub

front brake

spokes

Fig. 1.1. The parts of a mountain bike.

KNOW YOUR MOUNTAIN BIKE

The mountain bike has evolved quite a bit in recent years. The average mountain bike today is lighter, faster, and more comfortable than those of a decade ago, and even relatively cheap machines can be a pleasure to ride.

MOUNTAIN BIKE FEATURES

The most obvious developments have been in brakes and suspension. These days, many mountain bikes come with disk brakes, as opposed to various types of rim brakes, although amongst the latter, the V-brake is still quite common—and very effective. At the same time, front and rear suspension have become so ubiquitous that it's now difficult to find a mountain bike without at least the former.

Yet one thing applies to today's mountain bike at least as much as it did to yesterday's: its performance drops off sharply if it is not maintained properly. Your basically great modern bike deserves careful maintenance —and immediate repair if anything goes wrong. With the help of this book, that work will be easy and satisfying.

Fig. 1.2. Typical modern "hardtail" bike, this one equipped with disk brakes.

1

Before getting down to the actual maintenance and repair instructions, you should familiarize yourself with the bike and its components. You will be in a better position to evaluate and fix any problems once you know what the various parts are called, how they operate, and how they interact. That's what this chapter aims to explain, and to do so, I will "walk" you through the various functional component groups of the bike, explaining their operation along the way.

Of course, not all mountain bikes are created equal, and some of the components may differ from one model to the next. In this book, most of the illustrations and instructions will be based on a modern "standard" medium-quality mountain with front suspension and ei-

ther V-brakes or disk brakes. Other components are shown with the use of illustrations of other models: full-suspension bikes for the rear suspension parts, and older machines for operations involving the type of brakes that preceded the use of V-brakes and disk brakes. Since even a 15-year old bike can be perfectly good, and deserves to be kept functional, the book also covers the maintenance of such "outdated" components.

When you bought the bike, it probably came with a user's manual, which often contains helpful information, both with respect to bike handling and maintenance. Be alert for differences between your particular bike and the details described in such a manual, though, because it won't be written quite so specifically that all of it applies to the particular model you're dealing with.

There may also have been pull tags and/or instruction manuals for some of the components and accessories installed. Keep all these instructions with this book for reference when you experience problems with those specific parts.

PARTS OF THE MOUNTAIN BIKE

Fig. 1.1 shows a typical mountain bike with the names of the various components. To ease the process of describing these many parts, I will treat them in functional groups as follows:

Fig. 1.3. Full-suspension bike, also with disk brakes.

- frame
- wheels
- brakes
- drivetrain
- gearing system
- steering system
- seat and seatpost
- suspension
- accessories

In Chapters 3 through 18, the individual maintenance and repair instructions will be treated, arranged roughly on the basis of these same functional groups.

THE FRAME

Together with the front fork, the frame forms the frameset. Together, they can be considered the bike's backbone—the structure to which all the other components are attached, either directly or indirectly. Since most mountain bikes now have at least front suspension, the forks are usually suspension forks, and in many cases the frame itself may incorporate a suspension system for the rear.

Although different materials (which in turn allow for frames of different shapes) may be used on some bikes, most frames still comprise a tubular metal structure as shown in Fig. 1.4, or some variant of this general design (e.g., with non-round and/or varying cross-section tubes).

The front part, called main frame, is a trapezoidal structure of relatively thick tubes, called top tube, seat tube, down tube, and head tube respectively. The rear part, referred to as rear triangle, has roughly parallel pairs of thinner tubes, called seat stays and chain stays respectively, that meet at the point where the rear wheel is installed. On a full-suspension bike, the rear triangle is part of the suspension system and may have a shape that defies the "triangle" definition.

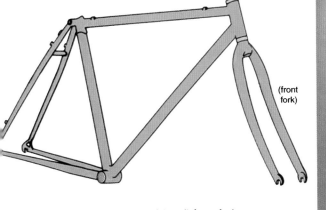

(front fork)

Above: Fig. 1.4. Frame and (rigid) front fork.

Right: Fig. 1.5. Typical (front) wheel.

1

Smaller parts are attached to the various tubes to hold other component: drop-outs, or fork-ends, to hold the wheels; brake bosses to hold the rear brake; a seat clamp to hold the seat; and the bottom bracket shell to hold the bearings for the cranks. The bearings for the steering system are installed in the head tube.

The frame is not usually a candidate for maintenance and repair work, but Chapter 15 covers all you will need to know about the frame.

THE WHEELS

After the frame, the wheels are the most important parts of the bicycle. Because they are also the most trouble-prone, their various aspects will be covered in Chapters 3, 4, 5, and 6.

As shown in Fig. 1.5, a wheel consists of the hub and a network of spokes connecting it to the rim, on which the tire and the inner tube are mounted. The hub runs on ball bearings and is held at the fork-ends at the front fork or dropouts at the rear triangle of the frame.

The tire is inflated by means of a valve that protrudes inward through the rim. Most wheels are held in by means of a quick-release mechanism, although they may also be held in by means of hexagonal axle nuts.

THE BRAKES

All mountain bikes are equipped with hand-operated brakes working on the front and rear wheels. Although today's high-end fashion calls for disk brakes, most bikes still use rim brakes. All these stop the bike by pushing a pair of brake pads against a metal surface: on disk brakes that's a separate disk, or "rotor," attached to the wheel hub, whereas they act on the sides of the wheel rim on rim brakes. Of the rim brake types, only the

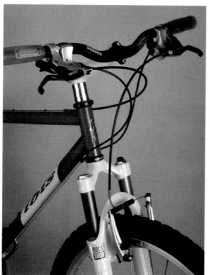

Left: Fig. 1.6. Brake lever and cable-operated V-brake.

Right: Fig. 1.7. Hydraulically operated disk brake.

V-brake design is currently in common use.

The brakes themselves are attached to the fork and the frame's rear triangle. Each brake is controlled by means of a lever mounted on the handlebars—one on the right for the rear brake, and one on the left for the front brake. A flexible cable or hydraulic tube connects the lever with the brake itself.

Depicted here in Fig. 1.6 and 1.7, chapters 7 and 8 cover work on rim brakes and disk brakes respectively.

The Gearing System

Chapter 9 deals with the derailleurs themselves and their controls. The derailleur system achieves changes of gear ratio, needed to adapt the rider's effort and pedaling speed to differences in terrain conditions, by moving the chain from one combination of front chainring and rear cog to another. Selecting a bigger chainring in the front or a smaller cog in the back results in a higher gear, e.g., for fast riding on a level road; selecting a smaller chainring or a larger cog provides a lower gear, e.g., for riding uphill. The number of available gears is calculated by multiplying the number of chainrings on the front by the number of cogs in the back—usually 27.

The gear-change operations are carried out by means of the front and rear derailleurs respectively (the one on the front is called changer in the UK, where the rear derailleur may be referred to as "mech," short for mechanism).

The derailleurs are controlled by means of shifters installed on the handlebars. The shifters are connected with the derailleur mechanisms by means of flexible cables.

The Drivetrain

Also known as the transmission, this is the group of components that transfers the rider's input to the rear wheel. Strictly speaking, the derailleur gearing

Fig. 1.8. Mountain bike drivetrain and derailleur gearing components.

1

system is also part of the drivetrain, but chapters 10—12 deal with the other components of the drivetrain.

What will be covered here are the cranks, the bottom bracket bearings, the pedals, the chain, and the chainrings (the large gear wheels attached to the right-hand crank).

Chapter 10 deals with the crankset, Chapter 11 with the chain, and Chapter 12 with the pedals.

THE STEERING SYSTEM

The steering system is quite critical for bike handling, whether riding in curves or following a straight course, but also for balancing the bike. It comprises the front fork, which holds the front wheel; the handlebars; the stem, which connects these two parts; and the headset, which allow the entire system to pivot in the frame's head tube.

Maintenance of the front fork, handlebars, stem, and headset is covered in Chapter 13, while the suspension fork is dealt with in Chapter 16, which is devoted to front suspension.

SEAT AND SEATPOST

Although perhaps the least glamorous part of the bicycle, the seat is quite important for comfort and control of the bike. It is held in place in the frame's seat tube by means of a seatpost, or seat pin, which is clamped in by means of a device called binder bolt. On many mountain bikes, this binder bolt takes the form of a quick-release mechanism,

Left: Fig. 1.9. Mountain bike steering system: handlebars, stem, headset, and front fork.

Above: Fig. 1.10. Seat and seatpost.

so the seat height is easy to adjust. Chapter 14 deals with these components.

SUSPENSION

Most modern mountain bikes come with some form of suspension. Chapters 16 and 17 deal with front and rear suspension-related maintenance issues respectively.

ACCESSORIES

1

Although none are shown in Fig. 1.1, there is a wide range of accessories available for the bicycle. For a mountain bike used under off-road conditions, it's best to keep the bike as uncluttered as possible. Such items as locks, reflectors, bicycle computers, luggage racks (carriers), and fenders (mudguards) are covered in Chapter 18.

Left: Fig. 1.11. Typical front suspension fork.

Above: Fig. 1.12. Close-up of typical rear suspension system.

2. PREVENTIVE MAINTENANCE

The best way to reduce the risk of accidental damage and the need for repairs is by means of regular preventive maintenance, ranging from cleaning to lubrication and adjustment of components.

MAINTENANCE SCHEDULE

I suggest you adhere to a three-part schedule, consisting of a quick pre-ride inspection and more extensive monthly and annual inspections, during which minor problems can be fixed before they become major problems.

Just as importantly, always be alert when riding the bike, so you notice anything that may go wrong along the way, and fix such problems at the first opportunity. For instance, if you accidentally hit a pothole hard while riding, do check the condition of tire and rim afterwards, and get them fixed if needed. And when you notice something is rattling, scraping, or rubbing as you ride, find out what the cause is and correct it right away.

Finally on this subject, where you keep the bike when you're not riding it is also important for its condition. Keep it out of the rain and direct sunlight as much as possible in a place where others can't interfere with it. If you have to keep it in a public or quasi-public place—whether that's in front of your place of work or in the back yard of an apartment building, always lock it to something fixed, using a long cable that goes through the frame and the wheels

Fig. 2.1. Hold the pump and the valve straight when inflating a tire.

as well as a large U-lock. If possible, even place a tarp over the bike—preferably one "tailored" for a bike, wrapping it all the way around to a point close to the ground.

PRE-RIDE INSPECTION

If you take the bike out several times on the same day, that may not be necessary each time you do, but it's a good idea to follow this procedure at least for the first ride on any day you ride the bike.

Of course, things don't go drastically wrong overnight. However, the cumulative effect of many days of riding are best dealt with on a daily basis—if it takes 10 days of use for something to vibrate loose, you'd probably not know to check it at the right time except by making it a daily routine.

TOOLS AND EQUIPMENT:

- Usually none required except any tools needed to make corrections.

PROCEDURE:

1. Check the quick-releases on the wheels and on the brakes to make sure they're in the closed position. The best check is to loosen them first and then tighten them. If they feel at all loose or if they don't require firm force to tighten, they're adjusted too loose. In that case, set the lever in the "open" position, tighten the thumb

nut by about one turn and tighten the lever again. Repeat if necessary.

2. Check operation of the brakes, which must be able to block rotation of the wheels when the levers are pulled to within ¾ inch (2 cm) from the handlebars. Do this by pulling each of the levers in turn while pushing down and forward on the bike at the handlebars for the front brake, and on the seat when testing the rear brake. Adjust the brakes if necessary.

3. Check to make sure the handlebars are straight and tight. To do that, straddle the front wheel, holding it tightly between your legs, and apply

Fig. 2.2. Checking the brake action.

force to the handlebars trying to twist them in the horizontal and vertical plane. Adjust and tighten if necessary.

4. Especially if others sometimes ride your bike too, check to make sure the seat is at the right height for you, straight, and firmly clamped in. Adjust and tighten if not.

5. Check whether the tires are inflated properly—at least to the pressure listed on the sidewalls. In the beginning, always use a pressure gauge; after some practice, you'll be able to

quickly feel by hand whether they're at least "about right."

6. Check operation of the gears by lifting the rear wheel off the ground and engaging each gear combination while turning the pedals. Adjust if necessary.

7. Rotate each wheel, while it is lifted off the ground, to check whether they turn smoothly, without interference or visible wobbling.

8. With the rear wheel lifted, turn the cranks to make sure the drive to the wheel works smoothly. Make any corrections that may be necessary.

Fig. 2.3. Checking the steering system.

MONTHLY INSPECTION

The monthly inspection consists of a more thorough check and some routine maintenance operations to make up for wear, but also to take care of the cleaning and preserving that is not necessarily due to actual use of the bike but simply to the "ravages of time." This inspection is best done in the workshop, if you have managed to arrange for one, whereas the daily inspection is easily done almost anywhere the bike happens to be at the time.

When carrying out this (or any other) inspection, be alert to any signs of damage in addition to those specifically mentioned here. Thus, you may find some part to be loose, cracked, or otherwise damaged. Fix or replace such items as soon as you notice them. Ask for advice at a bike shop, if you're not sure whether something is serious enough to warrant replacement.

PROCEDURE:

1. CLEANING

Clean the bike and apply protective coating as described under *Cleaning the Bike* starting on page 25.

2. LUBRICATION

Lubricate the following parts:

- The chain, spraying on a special chain spray lubricant available at a bike shop.
- Brake levers, shifters, pivot points of exposed mechanisms and cable ends, using thin spray lubricant and aiming carefully with the thin tubular nozzle extension provided.

Afterward, wipe off all excess lubricants to prevent parts of your bike becoming sticky and attracting dirt.

3. GENERAL CHECK

Follow all the steps described under *Pre-Ride Inspection* on page 17.

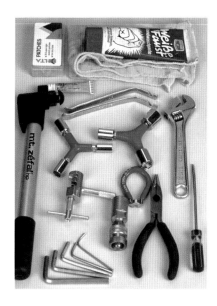

Above: Fig. 2.4. Selection of simple tools that will allow you to take care of most maintenance jobs at home and on the trail.

Left: Fig. 2.5. Checking the bottom bracket bearings.

4. HUB BEARINGS

Check the wheels for loose bearings (applying sideways force at the rim while holding the front fork for the front wheel, or the frame for the rear wheel)—if it moves, the bearings have to be adjusted as per Chapter 6.

5. RIM AND SPOKES

Check the wheels for wobble and loose, bent, or broken spokes. Wheel wobble is checked by lifting the wheel off the ground and looking at it from behind at a fixed point while rotating it. If it appears to wobble sideways or up-and-down as it turns, it needs to be "trued," following the instructions in Chapter 5, which also includes instructions for dealing with loose, bent, or broken spokes.

6. TIRES AND TUBES

Check the tires for damage and significant wear. Replace them if there are bulges, cuts, or seriously worn areas. Remove any embedded objects and replace the tube if it has been losing pressure from one day to the next. Make sure the valves are seated straight and the tires are seated equally deep all around the rims. Chapter 4 has all the relevant instructions.

7. BRAKES

Check the operation of the brakes and, if the bike has rim brakes, observe whether the brake pads (brake blocks) touch the rim squarely over their entire length and width when you pull the brake lever to within about ¾ inch (2 cm) from the handlebars. Adjust if nec-

Left and above: Figs. 2.6 and 2.7. Two ways of working on the bike, using a repair stand or simply placed upside down—cheap but fine if you protect anything mounted on the handlebars.

essary, referring to the instructions in Chapters 7 and 8.

8. Cranks

Using either the wrench part of the crank tool or a fitting Allen wrench (depending on the crank attachment detail), tighten the bolts that hold the cranks to the bottom bracket spindle. You may have to remove a dust cap first, and re-install it to protect the internal screw thread.

9. Accessory check

Inspect any accessories installed on the bike, as well as any you keep at home for occasional use. Make sure they are in operating order, and fix them if not. Tighten the mounting hardware for anything installed on the bike.

10. Final check

Carefully go over the entire bike and check to make sure all nuts and bolts are in place and tightened, nothing is loose, and no parts are missing or damaged. Make any corrections necessary.

2

ANNUAL INSPECTION

This is essentially a complete overhaul, to be carried out after a year's intensive use. If you ride in really bad weather and muddy terrain a lot—like real mountain biking—I'd even encourage you to carry out this inspection twice a year, once each at the end of summer and the end of winter. Proceed as outlined below.

Fig. 2.8.
Lubrication
points.

2

PROCEDURE:

1. PRELIMINARY WORK

Clean the bike and then carry out all the work described above for the pre-ride inspection and the monthly inspection.

2. VISUAL INSPECTION

Carefully check over the entire bike and all its components and accessories noting any damage, and correct anything that appears to be wrong before proceeding, following the relevant instructions in the appropriate chapters—or referring the work to a bike shop.

3. WHEELS

For each wheel (still on the bike), check all around the tire and the rim for any signs of damage or serious wear, as well as bent or broken spokes, and correct anything found amiss, following the instructions in Chapters 4 and 5. Then remove the wheel from the bike and overhaul the wheel hubs, referring to the instructions in Chapter 6 (if the hubs have adjustable bearings). If the hubs have cartridge bearings, thoroughly clean the surfaces and note any signs of rough operation or looseness, in which case you should replace those bearings completely, either using a special tool or entrusting that work to a bike mechanic.

Left: Fig. 2.9. An assortment of Lubrication and cleaning aids.

Above: Fig. 2.10. Lubricating a ball bearing using bearing grease..

4. CHAIN

Remove the chain and clean it thoroughly by washing it in a container with solvent, using a brush, then letting it dry over the used solvent bath and rubbing it with a cloth.

Check for apparent chain "stretch" (actually, the effect of wear). To do that, you can either use a special chain length gauge or measure the length of a 50-link section. On a new chain, that should measure 25 inches (63.7 cm), and any greater length is a sign of wear. Since 2 percent is the maximum allowable wear, replace the chain if the 50-link section measures more than 25½ inches (65 cm). Instructions for this work can be found in Chapter 11.

5. BOTTOM BRACKET

With the cranks still attached to the bottom bracket spindle, check to make sure there is no sideways play, which would indicate loose bearings. Then remove the cranks, following the instructions in Chapter 10, and spin the bottom bracket spindle to make sure it rotates smoothly.

If there is any sign of wear or looseness, take the bearings apart, clean and lubricate them, and adjust them (if it's an adjustable type, done from the right-hand side) or replacing the bearings (if they're of the cartridge type). Finally, reassemble the bottom bracket and the cranks, again following the instructions in Chapter 10.

2

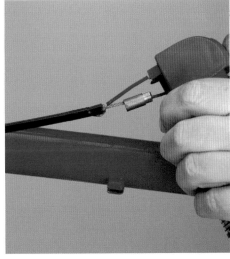

Left: Fig. 2.11. Lubricating derailleur pivot points.

Above: Fig. 2.12. Lubricating gear and brake cables.

2

6. PEDALS

Turn the pedals, and check to make sure they turn freely but without play and they don't wobble as you rotate them (which would be a sign of a bent spindle). If anything is not right, remove the pedals and disassemble them to clean, lubricate and adjust or replace the bearings and replace any damaged parts, following the instructions in Chapter 12.

7. STEERING

Check the operation of the headset as described above for the monthly inspection. If there is any sign of looseness or rough operation, overhaul it. See the instructions for overhauling the headset in Chapter 13.

Fig. 2.13. Cleaning in tight spots.

8. GEARING

While the chain is removed for the work per step 4 above, thoroughly clean, check, and lubricate all the components of both derailleurs (if the bike has derailleur gearing), making sure the pivots operate smoothly and the little wheels, or pulleys, over which the chain normally runs turn freely (unlike all other rotating parts on the bike, in their case, it's normal that they have sideways play). Fix or replace any problematic parts as explained in Chapter 9.

9. CONTROLS

Remove the control cables for both the gearing and the brakes. Clean them, replace them if there is any damage (such as broken strands near the nipple or frayed ends on the inner cable, or kinks in the outer cable). Then rub wax onto the inner cable and reinstall the cables, referring to Chapters 7, 8, and 9 for rim and disk brakes and gears respectively.

While the cables are removed, inspect the shifter and the brake lever for smooth operation, at which time you will also have a better chance to clean and lubricate the moving parts of these devices.

After you have reinstalled the cables, check the operation of the system and make any adjustments that may be necessary, again referring to the relevant chapters 7, 8, and 9 for brakes and gearing respectively.

10. ACCESSORIES

If you have any accessories for the bike—whether permanently installed or not—this is the time to check their condition and operation, and take any corrective action that may be needed. Also check on any spare parts you have for the bike and/or its accessories. For example, if the spare tube you carry or keep at home has been used on the bike, make sure it is either repaired properly or replaced by a new one.

Similarly, spare bulbs or batteries for a lighting system should be checked and replaced if necessary. Finally, check the contents and condition of your tool kit and replace anything that's found wanting (e.g., the rubber solution and the patches in the tire repair kit have a limited life even if not used, and should be replaced with new ones once every two years).

2

CLEANING THE BIKE

Although it's recommended to clean your bike once a month, it may have to be done more frequently if you ride in wet and dirty terrain a lot—in fact, after every such ride. Depending on the weather and the terrain, the nature of the dirt can be quite different.

Where I live, in Northern California, we encounter about 8 months of dry, dusty conditions, and 4 months of possibly wet, muddy ones. During the wet period, it's important to avoid corrosion and thus necessary to use wax and lubricants rather generously. However, when it's dry and dusty, open lubricated parts

Left: Fig. 2.14. Cleaning and polishing paint of frame.

Right: Fig. 2.15. Cleaning between cogs.

are actually a hazard because of their tendency to hold fine dry dust particles that work like an abrasive, causing wear and rough operation of moving parts and controls.

Keep such points in mind, while otherwise generally following the following procedure.

PROCEDURE:

1. If the bike is dry, wipe it clean as much as possible with a soft brush or a clean cloth to remove any loose dust. If the bike is wet or the dirt is caked on, clean the bike with a bucket full of water and a sponge. Don't use a hose with a strong spray

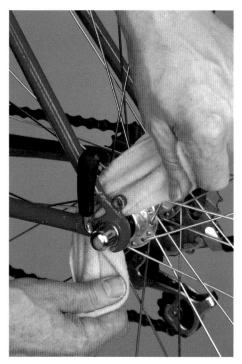

Fig. 2.16. Cleaning around the hubs.

nozzle, to avoid getting water into the bearings and other sensitive parts. After washing the frame itself, take each of the other components and thoroughly clean around them.

2. Use a clean, dry cloth to dry off all the parts that got wet in the preceding operation.

3. Next, use a solvent-soaked cloth to clean the small, hidden corners of the bike and its components and accessories—from the areas around the spokes to those behind the brakes and the nooks and crannies of the derailleurs. Many of the smallest corners are best reached by wrapping the cloth around a thin, narrow object, such as a screwdriver, while the way to get between or behind the cogs and the chainrings is by folding the cloth and pulling it back-and-forth from both sides.

4. To protect the areas you've just cleaned under step 3, do the same with a cloth soaked in lubricant or wax (use wax for dry weather, especially if it will be dusty, and oil if the weather and the terrain are more likely to be wet).

You can combine steps 3 and 4 by soaking the cloth in a mixture of solvent with about 10 percent oil. However, don't use this on any parts that come in contact with seals, such as suspension parts and hydraulic brake controls. In those applications, use only non-mineral-oil cleaners, as available form the component manufacturers.

5. Treat all painted and unpainted metal surfaces of the bike and its parts with wax. If the paint or the

Fig. 2.17. Cleaning inside a clipless pedal.

metal surfaces appear to be weathered, you can use an automotive liquid wax that contains an abrasive compound, otherwise regular automotive wax is the material to use. Ideally, you should remove the handlebar stem and the seatpost, so you can also treat the hidden portions of those parts. Reinstall them at the right height and orientation, and make sure they're held in place firmly, following the instructions in chapters 13 and 14respectively.

6. Rub out the wax coating with a clean, dry, soft cloth.

7. Treat all non-metallic surfaces, such as plastic (but not natural rubber, i.e., the tires), with Armor-All or a similar surface cleaner for plastic car parts. Rather than spraying it onto the bike, spray it onto a soft, clean cloth and rub it out.

3
Wheel Removal and Installation

Probably no other bicycle component requires more frequent maintenance than the wheels. This chapter provides detailed instruction for wheel removal and installation, while chapters 4–6 address maintenance of the wheel itself.

Wheel Installation

Most wheel and tire problems require the wheel to be removed from the bicycle. Although this may seem like a mundane task, it's an important enough one to warrant the detailed instructions given below. Actually, there are quite a number of different things to consider. It depends on many factors: whether it's

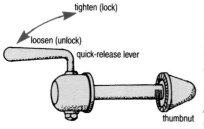

Left: Fig. 3.1. Quick-release operation.

Right: Fig. 3.2. A typical mountain bike wheel.

a front wheel or a rear wheel, whether it's held in with a quick-release or with axle nuts, and what kind of brake the bike has. For the instructions that follow, I've lumped most of those variables together, leaving us with two major categories and a special note: front wheel, rear wheel, and a note about wheels without quick-release.

REPLACE FRONT WHEEL

TOOLS AND EQUIPMENT:

- Usually none required
  Removal procedure:

1. If the bike has rim brakes. Open up the brake's quick-release or cable attachment to spread the brake arms

apart so the tire can pass between the brake pads. If he bike has disk brakes, the wheel can be removed without further preparation.

3

2. Twist the hub quick-release lever into the "open" position.

3. If the front fork has ridges at the end of the dropouts (common on most bikes sold in the U.S.), unscrew the thumbnut on the side opposite the lever until the hub can pass over them.

4. Slide the wheel out, guiding it at the hub and the rim.

INSTALLATION PROCEDURE:

1. If necessary, follow the same procedure as described in step 1 above for wheel removal, so the wheel will pass between the brake pads.

Above: Fig. 3.3. Quick-release lever in closed, or tightened, position.

Right: Fig. 3.4. Opening, or loosening, the quick-release lever.

3

2. Make sure the hub's quick-release lever is in the "open" position.

3. If there are ridges on the fork ends, unscrew the thumbnut far enough for the wheel to pass over them.

4. Slide the wheel over the fork ends, guiding it near the rim between the brake pads if the bike has rim brakes or at the disk if has disk brakes, until the hub is seated fully at the end of the slots in the fork ends.

5. Screw in the thumbnut until the lever can be tightened fully with significant hand force.

6. Center the wheel at the rim between the fork blades (leaving the same distance on both sides) by applying the brake, then tighten the quick-release lever.

7. Redo any attachments and adjustments that were affected by the removal of the wheel (see step 1 of the preceding *Removal procedure*).

REPLACE REAR WHEEL

TOOLS AND EQUIPMENT:

• Usually only a cloth to keep your hands clean while manipulating the chain.

REMOVAL PROCEDURE:

1. Shift the derailleurs into the gear that engages the smallest cog in the back and the smallest chainring in the front.

2. If the bike has rim brakes, open up the brake's quick-release or cable at-

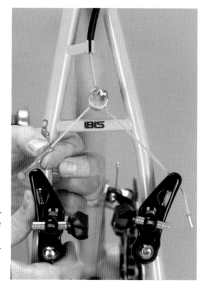

Left: Fig. 3.5. Opening up a V-brake to allow the tire to pass through.

Right: Fig. 3.6. Unhooking the straddle cable on a cantilever brake for the same purpose.

tachment to spread the brake arms apart, so the tire can pass between the brake pads. If there is no quick-release on the brake, you can either let the air out of the tire or undo the brake cable connection.

3. Hold back the derailleur with the chain as shown in Fig. 3.8 to provide a straight path, unobstructed by the routing of the chain around the derailleur pulleys.

4. Twist the hub quick-release lever into the "open" position.

5. Slide the wheel out, guiding it by the hub and at the rim.

INSTALLATION PROCEDURE:

1. If applicable, follow the instructions in step 1 of the *Wheel removal procedure*, so the wheel will pass between the brake pads.

2. Make sure the hub's quick-release lever is set to the "open" position.

3. Make sure the chain engages the smallest chainring in the front and the rear derailleur is set for the gear in which the chain engages the smallest cog, and route the chain over that smallest cog and around the pulleys as shown in Fig. 3.9.

4. Slide the wheel into the slot in the dropouts, guiding it near the rim between the brake pads if the bike has rim brakes, or at the disk if it has disk brakes.

3

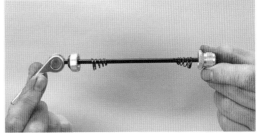

Above: Fig. 3.8. The conical springs on a quick-release spindle are placed at each end with the smaller-diameter end facing toward the hub.

Left: Fig. 3.7. Holding back the rear derailleur for rear wheel removal or installation.

5. Let go of the chain, routing it around the smallest cog and the derailleur pulleys as shown in Fig. 3.9.

6. Center the wheel at the rim between the seat stays (leaving the same distance on both sides) and tighten the quick-release lever. (If it can't be tightened fully or if it is too loose,

adjust the thumbnut until the lever can be tightened fully with significant hand force).

6. Redo any attachments and adjustments that were affected by the removal of the wheel (see step 1 of the *Removal procedure*).

WHEELS WITHOUT QUICK-RELEASE

On low-end bikes, even if the bike has a quick-release on the front wheel, there may be axle nuts used in the rear. In general, you can follow the same procedure for removal and installation as for a wheel with quick-release, but instead of undoing and tightening a quick-release lever, you'll have to unscrew the nuts on both sides with a fitting wrench.

Between the fork and the axle nut, there should be a flat washer, which must be replaced on the outside of the fork blade upon reassembly.

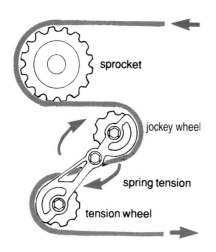

Above: Fig. 3.9. Chain routing around the cassette cogs on the rear wheel.

Left: Fig. 3.10. Closing, or tightening, the quick-release lever.

Right: Fig. 3.11. Loosening or tightening axle nuts on a wheel without quick-release.

TIRE MAINTENANCE

Probably no other part of the bicycle is more often in need of maintenance and repair than the tires. A puncture ("flat") is the most common mishap, but the tires need some regular maintenance as well.

THE TIRES

The type of tire used on mountain bikes is referred to as "clincher" in the U.S., "wired-on" in Britain. It fits around a separate inner tube and is held onto the rim by means of metal wires, or "beads" that are embedded in the sidewalls.

The tubes are equipped with a valve to control the air pressure, and two dif-

Left: Fig. 4.1. When inflating the tire, keep the valve perpendicular to the rim and the pump perpendicular to the valve.

Right: Fig. 4.2. Discard a tire if it has been damaged like this.

4

ferent valve types are in use—Presta ("French") and Schrader ("auto"). Make sure the pump matches that type of valve, because the use of adapter nipples is very cumbersome.

Tires are designated by their nominal size, which can be given in one of several methods. In the U.S., the most common one reads something like 26 x 1.75, meaning the tire is approximately 26 inches in diameter and about 1¾ inches wide. More critical, though is the ETRTO designation, which is also provided, be it in small print, on the tire sidewall. It will read something like 559

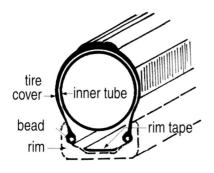

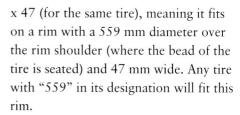

x 47 (for the same tire), meaning it fits on a rim with a 559 mm diameter over the rim shoulder (where the bead of the tire is seated) and 47 mm wide. Any tire with "559" in its designation will fit this rim.

Make sure you get tires that fit the rims and watch out to get a width that is small enough to clear the fork and the stays on your bike in the front and the rear respectively. Finally, some tire patterns are directional, in which case it should be installed so that the arrow points in the direction it rotates (spin the wheel the way it would turn when riding to verify which way that is).

Concerning the inner tube, other than the valve type, the size is also important, though not as critical as it is for the tire cover. Check the size range for which it is recommended before you buy one. Inner tubes have a limited shelf life (they are much more sensitive to time,

Above: Fig. 4.3. Tire and tube as installed on the rim.

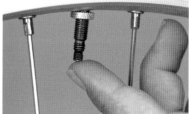

Left: Fig. 4.4. Inner tube rolled up to carry as spare.

Right: Fig. 4.5. On a Presta valve, unscrew the round nut at the tip and push the pin in briefly before placing the pump on it.

heat, and humidity than the tire covers seem to be), so don't buy a large supply of them at once, but rather buy just two at a time and replace them whenever you have to discard an existing tube due to age, number of patches, or porosity (when it starts losing air even though you can't identify a specific hole). They are available in different materials, and I like the very flexible ones made of pure latex (i.e., unvulcanized rubber) best—amongst other things because they are easier to patch than the ones made of butyl.

There are also special tubeless tires available, which also require special matching rims, but they are so rare that their maintenance and repair are not covered in this book.

TIRE INFLATION

Actually, you don't inflate the tire but the tube. Inflate it whenever the pressure is inadequate (anything less than the pressure marked on the sidewall is inadequate), and it's usually safe to inflate up to about 30 psi, or 2 bar, more than that figure for better tire life, if you can live with the harder ride.

4

TOOLS AND EQUIPMENT:

- pump
- pressure gauge, if available

PROCEDURE:

1. Make sure you have the right type (for Presta or Schrader valves) of

Above: Fig. 4.6. Pushing the tire sidewalls toward the (deeper) center of the rim by hand.

Right: Fig. 4.7. Inserting the first tire lever.

pump and pressure gauge for the type of valve on the tire.

2. Check whether the valve is straight in the rim (if it isn't, let all the air out, straighten it out by manipulating the tire sidewall at the same time as the valve).

3. Remove any dust cap that may be screwed on the end of the valve.

4. Depending on the type of valve:
   • If you're dealing with a Presta valve, unscrew the little round nut at the end and briefly push in the pin in the end to which the nut is attached with your finger to loosen it, but try not to let too much air escape.
   • If the bike has a Schrader valve, briefly push in its internal pin to loosen it using a pointed object, but try not to let too much air escape.

5. Check the air pressure with the pressure gauge, if available (once you have enough experience, you'll have developed a "calibrated thumb" with which you can estimate the pressure reasonably accurately without such a tool).

6. Place the pump head squarely onto the valve, seated properly on the valve. If the pump has a toggle lever,

Above: Fig. 4.8. Two tire levers in place.

Right: Fig. 4.9. Removing the tire sidewall from the rim by hand.

flip it to camp the pump head around the valve more effectively.

7. Holding the pump perpendicular to the valve, inflate the tire to the desired pressure (if the pump does not have a built-in pressure gauge, check with the separate pressure gauge).

8. If the valve is of the Presta type, tighten the nut at the end, and reinstall the dust cap for either type of valve.

Inner Tube Replacement

The easiest and quickest way to "fix" a bike with a punctured tire is to replace the inner tube. However, since there's a limit to the number of inner tubes you're likely to take along, and for the sake of economy, I suggest you also learn how to actually repair a punctured tube, which will be described under *Puncture Repair*.

Before commencing, remove the wheel from the bike, following the instructions in Chapter 3.

Tools and equipment:

- set of tire levers (preferably 3 thin flat ones)
- tire pump for the type of valve installed on the bike
- pressure gauge for the same type of valve
- spare tube of the same type and size as is installed on the bike
- preferably some talcum powder to treat the new tube so it does not deteriorate or adhere to the inside of the tire cover
- sometimes a pair of tweezers to remove sharp embedded objects from the tire cover

Fig. 4.10. Checking the inside of the tire cover for damage.

PROCEDURE:

1. Remove the dust cap from the valve and let any remaining air out of the tire by pushing in the pin in the valve (after unscrewing the little round nut in the case of a Presta valve).

2. If there is a nut screwed onto the base of the valve, remove it.

3. Push the valve into the tire as far as possible to create more space for the tire bead toward the center of the rim.

4. Manipulate the tire sidewall by hand, working all around to push the bead toward the deeper center section of the rim, then work one area of the side from which you're working, some distance away from the valve, back up to the edge of the rim.

5. Place the end of the long part of the L-shaped tire lever under the tire bead over the top of the side of the rim, with the short end of the tire lever facing toward the center of the wheel. Then use it as a lever to push the bead of the tire up and over the side of the rim, hooking the notch in the short end of the lever onto a spoke.

6. Do the same with the second tire lever, about 4 spokes further to one side.

7. If necessary (i.e., if the tire sidewall can't be pushed off the rim by hand at this point), do the same with the third tire lever.

8. At this stage, you can remove the first tire lever you installed (and if

Above: Fig. 4.11. Placing the rim tape over the heads of the nipples in the rim bed, with the valve hole lined

Right: Fig. 4.12. Replacing the tube, starting at the valve.

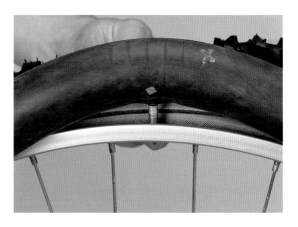

necessary, you can use it as a fourth lever, though that's rarely the case).

9. Remove the entire side of the tire cover off the rim by hand, working around gradually from the area where you used the tire levers.

10. Pull most of the inner tube out from between the tire cover and the rim.

11. Push the valve through the valve hole and remove the entire inner tube.

12. Check the condition of the tire cover inside and out, and remove any sharp embedded objects that may have been the cause of the puncture (using tweezers if you can't get them out by hand).

13. Check the condition of the rim tape that covers the deepest section of the rim bed to make sure it is intact and has the right width (it must just cover the deepest portion of the rim but not go up the sides) and no spoke ends are poking through (replace the rim tape and/or file off protruding spoke ends, as necessary).

14. Install the new tube, starting at the valve, carefully making sure it is embedded properly in the deepest section of the rim under the tire.

15. Inflate the tube just a little so it is no longer "limp" but without any significant pressure.

16. Starting at the valve, pull the tire cover back over the rim, working it into the deepest section of the rim as you work your way around in both directions until it is in place over its entire circumference.

   The last part will probably be tough, but don't use a tire lever or any other tool to do this—instead, achieve enough slack by working the bead deeper into the center section and pulling the entire tire toward the valve (you may have to let more air out of the tube), then pull the last section over from the opposite side as shown in Fig. 4.19.

17. Inflate the inner tube slightly and then "knead" the sidewalls until you're sure no part of the inner tube is caught in between the rim and the tire bead.

4

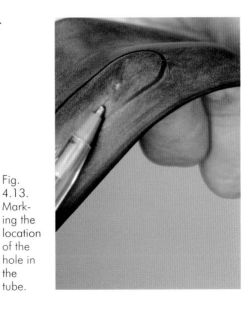

Fig. 4.13. Marking the location of the hole in the tube.

4

18. Inflate the inner tube to its final pressure, making sure the tube gets seated properly as you do so. It's seated properly if the ridge on the side is the same distance from the rim all around the circumference on both sides, and if necessary, correct it by first letting some air out, then "kneading" the tire, working all around until it is seated properly, and then re-inflating the tire.

19. Check the pressure with the pressure gauge and correct it if necessary.

Puncture Repair

If you don't have (any more) spare tires with you, or once you get home, you can usually repair a damaged inner tube by patching it. Most of the work is the same as what was described above for replacing the inner tube, so this description only covers the actual patching of the tire. To get to that stage when you have to do this by the roadside or whenever you have to repair the tube that's installed on the bike, first carry out steps 1 through 12 of the procedure *Inner Tube Replacement* above, using the tools listed there. And when you are done patching the inner tube, resume work at step 13 of that procedure.

Tools and equipment:

- tire patch kit (adhesive patches, sand paper or abrasive scraper, rubber solution, and talcum powder)

Procedure:

1. Check the entire surface of the tube, starting at any location you may have identified as the probable cause of

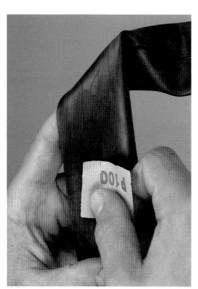

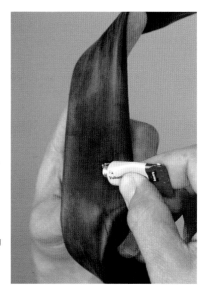

Left: Fig. 4.14. Sanding down the area to be patched.

Right: Fig. 4.15. Applying rubber solution to the tube.

the puncture on account of damage to the tire.

2. If you can't easily find the location of the leak, inflate the tube and pass it along your ear or your eye, to listen or feel where air escapes. If you don't find it this way, dip the inflated tube in a basin with water and watch for escaping air bubbles—that's the location of the (or at least one) hole. If you have dipped the tire, dry it before proceeding. Make sure you identify every leak, because there may be more than one. Mark their location by drawing a circle that's bigger than the patch you will be using around each one.

3. Rough up the area with the abrasive from the tire patch kit and wipe it clean.

4. Apply a thin, even layer of rubber solution to the area to be patched, slightly bigger than the patch you have selected, and let it dry for about 1 minute in hot weather, 2–3 minutes in cold weather—until the surface of the rubber solution becomes dull.

5. Pull one end of the protective layer (usually aluminum foil) from the patch without touching the adhesive side of the patch, and apply the patch to the treated area of the tube, centered on the hole, while pulling off the remainder of the protective layer.

6. Apply firm pressure to the entire patch for about a minute, squeezing it by hand and rubbing it e.g., with the handle of a screwdriver while supporting the tire.

7. Check to make sure the patch has adhered properly over its entire surface

4

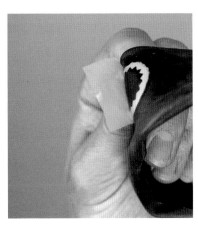

Left: Fig. 4.16. Applying the patch.

Right: Fig. 4.17. Placing the tube under the tire before installing the tire.

4

(and redo steps 3 through 6 if it has not).

8. Sprinkle some talcum powder over the patched area to prevent it from adhering to the inside of the tire cover. (Leaving the transparent plastic on the non-adhesive side of the patch has the same effect.)

9. Inflate the tube and wait about a minute to make sure it is not leaking, and if it is, repeat the repair for the same or any other hole you find.

10. Let the air out again and reinstall the tube under the tire cover over the rim as outlined in steps 13 through 19 of the procedure *Inner Tube Replacement*.

NOTE:

Make sure the rim tape is installed properly in the middle of the rim, covering the spoke nipples, and replace it if it is damaged or missing.

TIRE COVER REPAIR

Occasionally, you may be able to patch a tire cover if it has a small cut in it. However, it will be better to replace the tire completely if you can. If you do choose to patch it, follow the instructions above for tube repair and patch the inside cover with a small section cut from an old, thin tire. You'll have to use rubber solution on both the inside of the tire and on the patch. Sprinkle some talcum powder over the patch to prevent adhesion of the tire cover to the tube.

TIRE COVER REPLACEMENT

When a tire cover is worn or damaged, it too has to be replaced. Make sure it has the right size, corresponding to the rim size. For mountain bike use, some

Left: Fig. 4.18. Placing the tube under the tire before installing the tire.

Above: Fig. 4.19. Pulling the tire bead over the edge of the rim.

tires are marked with a direction of rotation and sometimes there are different tires recommended for front and rear use. Pay attention to those details and make sure you get the right type and install it the right way round. (To get the right direction of rotation, visualize the tire on the bike, with the chain on the right—the top of the tire will rotate forward as you look down on it.) The description is based on the wheel being removed from the bike.

TOOLS AND EQUIPMENT:

• set of 3 tire levers
• pump
• pressure gauge
• talcum powder

PROCEDURE:

1. Treat the inside of the new tire cover with talcum powder to prevent it adhering to the inner tube.

2. Deflate the inner tube and remove the tire cover and the inner tube as described in steps 1 through 11 of the procedure *Inner Tube Replacement*.

3. Put one side of the new tire cover over the side of the rim and push it into the center, making sure it faces the right way round if it's marked for a direction of location.

4. Put the inner tube back under the tire cover and then mount the other side of the tire cover over the rim, followed by a check and tube inflation in accordance with steps 13 through 18 of the procedure *Inner Tube Replacement*.

4

Fig. 4.20. Inflating the tire with a floor pump.

5 RIM AND SPOKE MAINTENANCE

Each wheel consists of a hub and a rim, with a set of spokes connecting them, and a tire with inner tube around the rim. This chapter deals with the rim and the spokes, while the hub is covered in Chapter 6.

RIM AND SPOKES

If a wheel gets damaged, it's likely to be the rim that takes the blow, and repair becomes a matter of either replacing the rim or straightening it. Both jobs require work with the spokes—either replacing them altogether or adjusting their tension to straighten the rim.

Left: Fig. 5.1. The wheel without the tire.

Right: Fig. 5.2. Parts of the wheel.

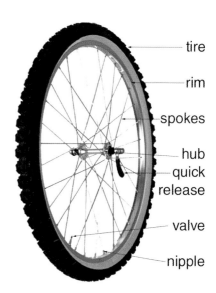

- tire
- rim
- spokes
- hub
- quick release
- valve
- nipple

Take a look at the way a bicycle wheel is built up. The usual way a wheel is built up is as shown in Fig. 5.1, while Fig. 5.2 shows the names of the individual components. On a typical mountain bike wheel, there are 32 spokes per wheel, half of which—every other one around the rim—run to the left-hand hub flange, the other half to the right-hand hub flange. The spokes on each side of the wheel provide radial and lateral (i.e., sideways) rigidity by pulling the rim in that direction, while the spokes on the other side pull in the opposite direction. Together, they balance the wheel both radially and laterally.

The spokes on each side of the wheel form a particular pattern (which is usually, though not always, the same on both sides). If they all run radially straight from the rim to the hub flange, it's called a radial pattern. If each spoke crosses one other spoke on the same side, it's called 1-cross; if it crosses two other spokes on the same side, it's called 2-cross, etc. Before you start work on a wheel, check the number of spokes and the spoking pattern, and if you replace any or all spokes, adhere to the same pattern. You will also need spokes of the same length (which is not necessarily the same on both sides) and thickness (referred to as "gauge").

Another thing to check before you get involved in wheel work is to check the spoke tension of a well-built new wheel. Do that by asking at a bike shop whether you can feel the spoke tension of a set of newly built wheels for a high-end bike. Check the spoke tension of the front wheel and both sides of the rear wheel by squeezing a pair of neighboring spokes together and noticing the resistance. Then "pluck" them like musical strings and note the pitch—higher tension results in a higher pitch. When maintaining or rebuilding a wheel, aim for the same spoke tension.

5

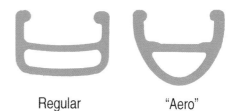

Regular   "Aero"

Above: Fig. 5.3. Rim cross-sections.

Right: Fig. 5.4. The parts used to build a wheel: spokes, nipples, rim, and hub. Also shown are the tools needed: spoke wrenches.

THE RIM

Bicycle rims for mountain bikes are always of one of the patterns shown in Fig. 5.3, although their depth and width may vary greatly. The inward-facing bulges at the tip of the sides serve to hook the bead of the tire into place.

The rim diameter must match the tire size—typically mountain bikes have 559 mm rims. The width may vary from quite narrow (like 22 mm) for a modern bike with disk brakes to very wide (like 30 mm) for some older mountain bikes.

The number of spoke holes must match the number of spokes in the wheel and on the hub. Finally, the valve hole must be the right size (for Presta or Schrader valves respectively).

WHEEL TRUING CHECK

Wheel damage usually originates with a blow to the rim, deforming it either radially or laterally. When it is deformed this way, it's called "out of true," and the trick is to get it "trued" again. As a result of the deformation, some of the spokes become looser and others tighter.

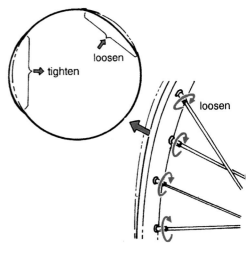

Radial truing

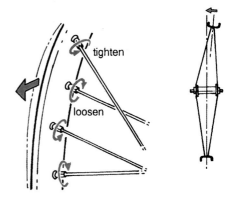

Lateral truing

Left: Fig. 5.5. View of nipples and spoke ends in the rim, with rim tape removed. The "empty" hole is the valve hole.

Above: Fig. 5.6. Wheel truing diagram.

Often, though not always, the damaged can be repaired by selective re-tensioning of the spokes. The first thing to do is to check the extent of the damage.

Tools and Equipment:

- Usually none required, although a wheel truing stand, preferably with built-in gauges, makes the job easier.

Procedure:

1. Place the bike in the repair stand or place it upside down (protecting any items mounted on the handlebars if necessary). Or, if you do have a wheel truing stand, remove the wheel and mount it in the truing stand.

2. Slowly spin the wheel by hand and observe the distance between each side of the rim and the frame or the truing stand. Observe whether the wheel wobbles either sideways, in which case it's laterally out of true, or radially (the outside of the wheel seems to wobble up-and-down as it rotates), in which case it's radially out of true. Also check whether any of the spokes are broken.

3. If there appears to be a gradual deformation over a significant area, you will probably be able to fix it by either radial or lateral truing, described below under *Wheel Truing*.

4. If there is a short, sudden deformation of the side of the rim, that is probably due to direct-impact damage of the rim, which cannot be repaired satisfactorily, and should be solved by replacing the entire rim, described under *Wheel Spoking/Rim Replacement* on page 52.

5. If inspection of the wheel reveals that one or more of the spokes are broken, they must be replaced, which is described under *Individual Spoke Replacement* on page 51, after which the wheel has to be trued as well.

Wheel Truing

This is the work necessary to get the wheel back into shape if your wheel truing check has established that it wobbles either sideways (i.e., it is laterally out of

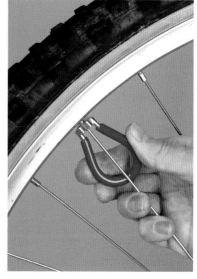

Fig. 5.7. Using a spoke wrench (nipple spanner) to adjust the spoke tension.

true) or up-and-down (i.e., it is radially out of true).Tools and equipment:

- spoke wrench
- if possible, truing stand, although it can be done using the bike's frame or front fork instead for rear wheel and front wheel respectively
- adhesive tape or chalk for marking
- sometimes penetrating oil and cloth

LATERAL TRUING PROCEDURE:

1. On the basis of the wheel truing check described above, mark (e.g., with pieces of adhesive tape wrapped around the nearest spokes or chalk marks on the tire) which section of the wheel is too far to the left or the right relative to the center between the two sides of the truing stand or either the frame's seat stays (for the rear wheel) or the front fork blades (for the front wheel).

2. In the area thus marked, loosen the spokes that lead to the same side as to which the buckle deviates from the center and tighten the spokes that run to the other side. Do this by turning the nipples with the spoke wrench—about one turn at the highest point of the buckle and gradually less to ¼ turn to the ones near the end of the buckled portion.

   Looking from the center of the wheel toward the rim, loosening is achieved when you turn clockwise, and tightening when you turn counterclockwise.

   If the spokes are corroded solidly in the nipples, so the nipples won't turn properly, spray some penetrating oil at the points where the spokes disappear into the nipples—and wipe off any excess—then wait 2–3 minutes before trying again.

3. Repeat step 2 (but turning the nipples less and less as you get closer to the desired effect) until the sideways wobble is eliminated (i.e., the wheel is laterally true).

RADIAL TRUING PROCEDURE:

Using the same techniques as described in step 1 of the preceding *Lateral truing*

Fig. 5.8. Using a truing stand.

procedure, identify the "flat spot" or the "high spot" of the rim by marking the nearest spokes. Then loosen the spokes in the "flat" area and tighten the ones in the "high" area until the up-and-down wobble, or "hop," is eliminated (i.e., the wheel is radially true), proceeding as in steps 2 and 3 of the preceding *Lateral truing procedure*.

EMERGENCY BUCKLED WHEEL REPAIR

If the damage occurs suddenly during a ride in the form of a badly buckled ("pretzeled") wheel, e.g., as a result of hitting an obstacle, you may be able to make a provisional repair by the roadside. Ride very carefully after this, because the wheel may suddenly collapse on you if you ride too fast in corners. Once you get home, do a thorough inspection and repair, which may well mean rebuilding or replacing the entire wheel.

TOOLS AND EQUIPMENT:

• spoke wrench

PROCEDURE:

1. Remove the wheel from the bike.

2. Find a suitable step, such as a curb stone, on which you can support one

5

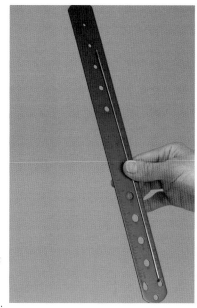

Right: Fig. 5.10. Use of spoke length gauge.

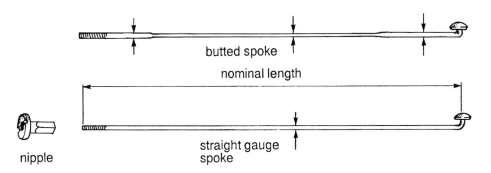

butted spoke

nominal length

straight gauge spoke

nipple

Fig. 5.9. Spoke detail drawing.

part of the rim while the other part is supported at a lower point and the hub axle stays clear of the road surface. Place the wheel in such a way that the most severe part of the outward deformation faces down on the higher support point.

5

3. Carefully but forcefully push down on the sections of the rim that are 90 degrees offset either side of the buckled portion. Continue or repeat until the rim is reasonably straight.

4. Place the wheel back in the bike and do a truing check as described above, then adjust the spoke tension as well as possible under the circumstances until the wobble is minimized.

5. Ride home carefully and do a more thorough check and repair or replacement.

THE SPOKES

Spokes are measured in mm as shown in the illustration, i.e., from the inside of the bend to the tip of the screw-threaded end. They are available in a wide array of sizes for different combinations of hub, rim, and spoking pattern. Their thickness is also measured in mm, while the nipples must be matched with the spoke thickness and screw thread.

These days, most spokes are made of stainless steel. Often spokes have different thicknesses in different sections. This is referred to as "butted" meaning that the ends (butts) are thicker than the middle section—a little lighter and more flexible, reducing the chance of breakage.

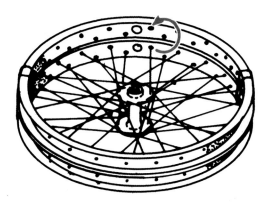

Above: Fig. 5.11. Drawing showing how the spokes are transferred from the old rim to the new one.

Right: Fig. 5.12. Transferring spokes from the old rim to the new rim.

Individual Spoke Replacement

This is necessary if one or more of the spokes are broken, usually at the bent portion near the head of the spoke, where it is attached to the hub flange. Replace broken spokes as soon as possible, because if you ride with one broken spoke, there is a great likelihood of additional wheel damage and more spokes breaking. Do this work with the wheel removed from the bike.

Note:

To gain access to the spoke holes in the hub flange, you may need to remove the brake disk or the rear cog set (cassette) first, following the instructions in chapters 8 and 9 respectively.

Note:

On some rims, the spoke holes are not reinforced with a ferrule, in which case there should be a little washer between the rim and the head of the nipple. When replacing spokes and nipples on a rim like that, don't forget to reinstall the washers.

Tools and equipment:

- spoke wrench
- cloth and a speck of lubricant
- sometimes, tire levers and pump

Procedure:

1. Remove the remaining piece (or pieces) of the broken spoke, unscrewing the outside portion from the nipple.

2. Buy a spoke that's exactly the same length and thickness as the other spokes on the same side of the wheel.

   If the spoke seems very loose in the nipple, you should also replace the nipple. Do that by removing a section of the tire and the tube as described in Chapter 4, lifting the rim tape, and prying out the old nipple.

5

Fig. 5.13. Checking wheel centricity.

Then insert the new one and reinstall the rim tape, the tube, and the tire.

3. Check to see how the spokes in the second hub flange hole from the spoke to be replaced run—whether the head is on the inside or the outside of the hub flange and whether it goes over or under the crossing spokes.

4. Apply a little lubricant to the threaded end of the spoke and then route the new spoke the same way as the one you observed in step 3, screwing the nipple onto the screw-threaded end of the spoke until it has the same tension as other spokes on the same side of the wheel.

5. Check the wheel as described above under *Wheel Truing Check* and make

any truing corrections as may be necessary following the description.

WHEEL SPOKING / RIM REPLACEMENT

Normally, this is a rather involved job that takes lots of practice to do effectively (or lots of time until you have lots of practice). For that reason, I recommend a simple procedure of unhooking the spokes on one rim and installing them into the new rim as you go along.

This method only works if you are replacing the rim by an identical rim (which means that you won't need to use new spokes of different length nor to replace the spokes and the hub.

If you have to replace the spokes or the hub as well, I recommend you entrust a bike mechanic with the work instead. Before starting with this work, remove the wheel from the bike (see Chapter 3) and remove the tire and the tube from the rim (see Chapter 4).

TOOLS AND EQUIPMENT:

*   spoke wrench (nipple spanner)
*   if possible, truing stand, although it can be done using the bike's frame or front fork instead for rear wheel and front wheel respectively
*   adhesive tape
*   lubricant and cloth
*   sometimes penetrating oil

Fig. 5.14. Wheel with 3-cross spoking pattern.

Procedure:

1. If applicable, remove the brake disk and/or the rear cogs (cassette) from the hub, following the procedures in chapters 8 and 9 respectively.

2. Place the new rim on top of the old one and align the valve hole of the new rim with that of the existing one, while checking whether they are indeed identical in size, depth, and hole pattern.

3. Tape the two rims together in two or three spots between spoke holes.

4. Starting at the spoke next to the valve hole and working around the circumference of the wheel, undo one spoke at a time by unscrewing the nipple. Then lubricate the screw-threaded end of the spoke. Finally install the nipple in the corresponding spoke hole on the new rim and screw the nipple onto the spoke. If the nipples are too tightly on the spokes, apply some penetrating oil to all the spoke ends at the nipples first and wait 2–3 minutes before trying to unscrew them.

5. When all the spokes are attached to the new rim, remove the old rim and then proceed by checking the wheel for lateral and radial true and making any adjustments necessary as described under *Wheel Truing Check* and *Wheel Truing* respectively.

5

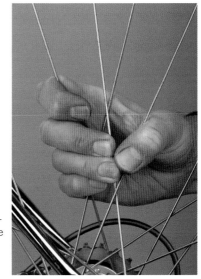

Fig. 5.15. Relieving spoke stress after the nipples are tightened fully.

6   HUB MAINTENANCE

Finally, among the chapters dealing with the various aspects of the mountain bike's wheels, this chapter covers maintenance of the hub, the central part of each wheel.

The hub consists of an axle, a set of ball bearings, and the hub body. On the sides, the hub body has flanges to accommodate the holes through which the spokes are inserted. Quick-release hubs have hollow axles, while they are solid for "bolted-on" hubs (more accurately "nutted," though that term is rarely used).

The ball bearings may be either adjustable cup-and-cone bearings or "sealed" cartridge bearings. The hub body is usually made of aluminum alloy. The number of spoke holes in the flanges must correspond to the number of spokes in the wheel, each flange usu-

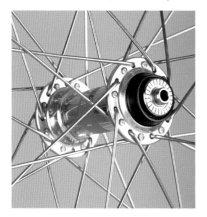

Above: Fig. 6.1. Close-up of a front wheel hub installed in the wheel.

Right: Fig. 6.2. Details of conventional hub with cup-and-cone bearings.

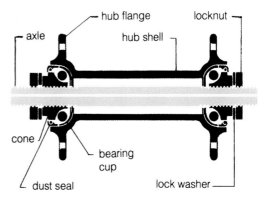

ally (but not always) holding half the total number of spokes.

Hub maintenance consists of adjusting, lubricating, overhauling, or replacing the bearings, although in rare cases the axle may have to be replaced as well. All this work can be done with the wheel left assembled, whereas replacing the hub requires rebuilding the entire wheel.

HUB BEARING CHECK

Do this work in conjunction with the annual overhaul—and whenever you detect symptoms of wear, such as high resistance or looseness of the wheel.

TOOLS AND EQUIPMENT:

• Usually none required

PROCEDURE:

1. No need to remove the wheel from the bike. First check to make sure the wheel is held into the frame or the front fork firmly, referring to the instructions in Chapter 3 to tighten it in case it is not.

2. Check whether the wheel turns freely by lifting the wheel off the ground and spinning it slowly by hand. If it continues to rotate and see-saws until finally coming to rest with the valve down, it's running smoothly enough. If not, the bearings must be adjusted or replaced.

3. Check whether there is play in the bearings, i.e., whether they are too loose, by holding the bike at the front fork (for the front wheel) or he frame (for the rear wheel) and trying to move the rim sideways relative to this point. If it can be moved

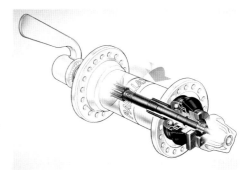

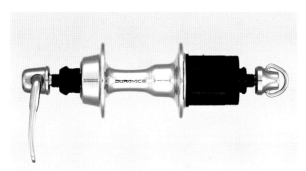

Above: Fig. 6.4. Manufacturer's cross-section drawing of a typical front hub (Shimano).

Left: Fig. 6.3. Manufacturer's illustration of a typical rear hub (Shimano).

loosely, the bearings are too loose and must be adjusted or replaced.

HUB BEARING ADJUSTMENT

This procedure only applies to hubs with cup-and-cone bearings. If the hub has cartridge bearings, refer to the instructions *Cartridge Bearing Maintenance* on page 59.

TOOLS AND EQUIPMENT:

- cone wrenches
- open-ended wrenches or combination wrenches

PROCEDURE:

1. Remove the wheel from the bike, as described in Chapter 3.

2. If there are neoprene boots covering the ends of the hub, first pry them off with a small screwdriver to gain access to the bearings.

3. While holding the cone firmly on one side with a cone wrench, loosen the locknut on the same side by about one full turn, using either another cone wrench or a regular wrench.

4. Lift the keyed washer that's installed between the cone and the nut so it comes loose from the cone.

5. Adjust the bearing:
    • If the bearing was too loose, tighten the cone about ⅛ turn at a time, while holding the locknut on the opposite side steady with a wrench.

Left: Fig. 6.5. Cleaning around a hub.

Right: Fig. 6.6. Adjusting a bearing cone on a hub with cup-and-cone bearings.

• If the bearing was too tight, loosen the cone about ⅛ turn at a time, while holding the cone on the opposite side steady with another cone wrench.

6. Tighten the locknut, while holding the cone on the same side, then check the adjustment as described above and repeat the procedure, if needed, until the hub runs smoothly without sideways play. If you can't get it to run smoothly, overhaul the hub in accordance with the procedure *Hub Lubrication and Overhauling* below.

7. Reinstall the wheel on the bike, following the instructions in Chapter 3.

Above: Fig. 6.7. Close-up of bearing adjusting parts.

Right: Fig. 6.8. Tightening or loosening the locknut against the cone.

HUB LUBRICATION AND OVERHAULING

This is best done in conjunction with the annual inspection summarized in Chapter 2, or whenever a bearing problem can't be solved with adjustment as described above. On a rear wheel, start on the left-hand side of the wheel because the bearing on the chain side is usually not easily accessible.

6

TOOLS AND EQUIPMENT:

• cone wrenches
• open-ended or combination wrenches
• thin, flat object with leverage, e.g., narrow tire lever or wide screwdriver
• cleaning cloths
• solvent
• bearing grease

6

DISMANTLING PROCEDURE:

1. Remove the wheel from the bike and remove the quick-release or the axle nuts and washers.

2. Holding the cone on one side with one cone wrench, remove the locknut on the same side with another cone wrench or a regular wrench.

3. Lift off and remove the lock washer, noting that it has an internal tag, or "key," that slides in a groove that runs lengthwise in the axle. Also remove any other spacers and washers that may be installed between the cone and the locknut.

4. Place the wheel horizontally (the side you're working on facing up), with a cloth under the hub. Loosen and remove the cone, holding the cone on the opposite side with a cone wrench. Catch all the bearing balls in the cloth.

5. Pull the axle out of the hub, with the cone and the locknut still installed on the opposite side, again carefully catching the bearing balls in the cloth.

OVERHAULING, LUBRICATING, AND REASSEMBLY PROCEDURE:

1. Carefully pry off any plastic dust caps at the hub ends, using a thin flat object such as a tire lever (but preferably leave them in place if they are made of metal).

2. Thoroughly clean all parts—bearing balls, cones, axle, bearing races, and dust cap.

Above: Fig. 6.9. Removing the seal of a hub with cartridge bearing.

Right: Fig. 6.10. Cone removed, exposing the bearings.

3. Inspect all parts, especially the contact surfaces of bearing races, cones, and bearing balls. Replace any parts that show signs of roughness, grooves, pitting, or corrosion.

4. Check the axle to make sure it is still straight by rolling it over a smooth level surface (e.g., a table top)—replace it if it wobbles.

5. Fill the bearing cups with bearing grease and push the bearing balls in (if you're in doubt about the correct number of balls, it should be one less than what you could squeeze in at the maximum). Then reinstall the dust caps, if they had been removed.

6. Reinsert the axle from the same side as from which it was removed, guiding it carefully so the end does not push any bearing balls out of the bearing cups.

7. Holding the end of the axle to which the cone and locknut are still attached, install the other bearing cone until almost tight—there should be just a little play left in the bearings.

8. Place the keyed lock washer on the axle, aligning the key with the groove in the axle. Also install any other spacers and washers that may have been present between the cone and the locknut.

9. Install the locknut and tighten it firmly against the underlying cone.

10. Check to make sure the bearings are now adjusted to provide smooth rotation without looseness, or play—if not, adjust according to the preceding procedure *Hub Bearing Adjustment*.

11. Reinstall the wheel on the bike, following the instructions in Chapter 3.

CARTRIDGE BEARING MAINTENANCE

The "sealed" cartridge bearings used on many modern bikes require less maintenance because they are better protected against the intrusion of dirt, and the lubricant is better retained inside the bearings.

Fig. 6.11. Lubricating a cup-and-cone bearing hub.

To replenish the lubricant, which should be done once a year, proceed as follows:

6

TOOLS AND EQUIPMENT:

- narrow, thin, flat screwdriver for raising the seal
- squeeze bottle or can with SAE 60 mineral oil
- cloth
- tire lever or similar flat object for pushing the seal in

PROCEDURE:

1. Remove the wheel from the bike, following the instructions in Chapter 3.

2. Lift the neoprene seal that covers the accessible bearings up with the screwdriver.

3. While holding up the seal with the screwdriver, squirt some mineral oil past it into the bearing until it runs out the other side, catching all excess oil with the cloth, and wiping all parts clean afterwards.

4. Remove the screwdriver and push the seal back into place by hand or with the aid of a flat object, such as a tire lever.

5. To gain access to the hidden bearing inside the cassette of the rear wheel (right-hand, or chain side), the bearing on the left-hand side would have to be removed first, a job best left to a bike mechanic who has the right tools for that.

6. Also if the bearings are loose or cannot be made to operate smoothly with lubrication, they will have to be replaced by a bike mechanic using special tools.

7. Reinstall the wheel on the bike, following the instructions in Chapter 3.

Fig. 6.12. Lubricated bearing of hub with cup-and-cone bearings.

7 Rim Brake Maintenance

Although many modern high-end mountain bikes are equipped with hydraulically operated disk brakes, more moderately priced new machines and all older bikes have rim brakes.

Since about 1995, the common rim brake has been the so-called V-brake, replacing the cantilever brakes that was most common in the early days of mountain biking. This chapter deals with rim brakes, whereas disk brakes are covered in Chapter 8.

There's nothing inherently wrong with any of the various types of brakes, and the one isn't necessarily superior to the other. They can all be made to work equally effectively with the right maintenance, which is what this chapter is all about.

V-Brakes

The V-brake, also referred to as "direct-pull" or "linear-pull" brake, is the most commonly installed brake on mountain bikes. It consists of two brake arms that pivot around bosses installed directly on

the fork and the seat stays. The inner and outer cables pull the upper ends of

Fig. 7.1. V-brake and cable-operated brake controls.

the brake arms together and the brake pads are attached to the brake arms halfway between the pivot and the cable attachment point.

The inner cable is clamped directly to one brake arm, while the outer cable ends in a bent tubular piece (referred to as a "noodle") that sits in a clamp at-

tached to the other brake arm. This is the point to undo when you have to release the cable tension.

CANTILEVER BRAKES

Like the V-brake, cantilever brakes are mounted on bosses welded on the fork blades and the seat stays. The brake arms of the cantilever brake stick out

Left: Fig. 7.2. Close-up of V-brake.

Right: Fig. 7.4. Close-up of cantilever brake.

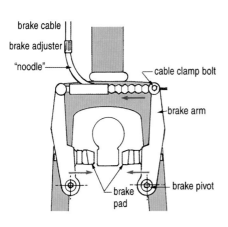

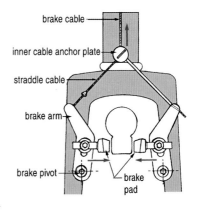

Above: Fig. 7.3. V-brake operation diagram.

Right: Fig. 7.5. Cantilever brake operation diagram.

more to the sides. Instead of the direct attachment of the cable to the top of the brake arms, the two brake arms, which are much shorter than they are on the V-brake, are connected by means of a straddle cable, which in turn is connected in the middle to the actual brake cable. The outer cable is held at a cable anchor attached to the frame some distance above the brake arms.

COMMON RIM BRAKE FEATURES

There are a couple of aspects that all rim brakes have in common, and these are the first, and most general, points to pay attention to when checking or maintaining the brakes.

Adjustability is usually provided either at the point where the cable comes out of the lever or at the point where the cable connects to the brake mechanism. Somewhere in the system is usually a quick-release device or some easily handled method of unhooking the inner or outer cable.

The most common adjustments are those of the brake pad position relative to the rim and the cable tension. The former adjustment assures that the brake pad wears evenly and works fully when engaged; the latter adjustment determines how quickly and consequently, how powerfully it can be engaged.

When working on the brakes, be aware that they should be treated as complete systems, including not only the brakes themselves, but also the brake levers, the control cables, and any attachments through which the cables run. In fact, even the condition of the rim and the spokes can influence brake performance.

7

Above: Fig. 7.6. This is how the brake pads should contact the rim.

Right: Fig. 7.7. Typical brake lever.

BRAKE TEST

To carry out the brake test suggested for the monthly inspection—or whenever you feel the need to verify the brake's efficacy, such as before a long tour—proceed as follows:

TOOLS AND EQUIPMENT:

• Usually none required, but please wear a helmet.

7

PROCEDURE:

1. Check to make sure the rims are clean, and if not, clean it with a slightly abrasive pad and water or mild solvent, followed by a dry cloth.

2. Check to make sure the brake pads are not excessively or irregularly worn, and replace them if they are.

3. Make sure the brakes themselves are firmly attached to the bike, the brake cable is firmly anchored and does not have any kinks, broken or frayed strands, and that the brake levers are firmly attached to the handlebars and can be easily reached.

4. For each brake (front and rear), check to make sure the brake pads touch the wheel rim parallel with the rim and with 1–2 mm clearance between the top of the brake pad and the edge of the rim. If not, make corrections as described under *Brake Adjustments* on page 66.

5. Check to make sure the brake pads touch the rim firmly when you depress the brake lever to within ¾ inch (2 cm) from the handlebars.

6. Get on the bike and ride it at a brisk walking speed (about 3–4 mph, or 5–

Left and right: Figs. 7.8 and 7.9. Two historic mountain bike brakes: roller cam brake (left) and U-brake (right). Nothing wrong with those designs, but they were replaced by the simpler V-brake and the more "high-tech"-looking disk brake.

7 km/h) on a clear, level paved surface, such as an empty parking lot. When doing the actual test, you must be going in a straight line.

FRONT BRAKE TEST PROCEDURE:

To test the front brake, apply the left-hand brake lever, gradually increasing hand force. If the bike starts to tip forward (i.e., the rear end of the bike starts lifting off the ground) once the brake is fully applied, the brake force is adequate. (Let go of the brake to prevent falling.)

If you can't get this to happen, the brake is not effective enough. Follow the procedure below to adjust the brake.

If the bike starts to tip forward almost immediately, the brake is grabbing too vigorously for controlled braking. Follow the procedures below to adjust the brake.

If the bike, or just the brake, vibrates, rumbles, or squeals when you apply the brake, it also needs attention as described below.

If applying the brake seems to require excessive force at the lever, there may be a problem with either the cable or the levers, and you are referred to the relevant sections below to correct this situation.

7

REAR BRAKE TEST PROCEDURE:

Proceed just as described above for the front brake test. However, the result will be different.

If you can apply the brake hard enough to make the rear wheel skid while the brake lever is pulled no closer than ¾ inch (2 cm) from the handlebars, it's powerful enough.

If you can apply the brake gradually enough to avoid skidding, you're lucky.

Above: Fig. 7.10. Adjusting the brake pads.

Right: Fig. 7.11. Adjusting the brake cable tension at the lever.

BRAKE ADJUSTMENTS

The following sections contain summaries of the various procedures to improve the performance of the brake when the brake test has revealed that something's not working quite right.

ADJUST BRAKE APPLICATION

Over time, brake pad wear, cable stretch, and pivot bushing wear in the various components combine to make the point where the brake lever activates the brake to get closer and closer to the point where the lever gets too close to the handlebars to apply sufficient force. As soon as it no longer applies powerful enough braking force when it is ¾ inch (2 cm) from the handlebars, it must be readjusted.

TOOLS AND EQUIPMENT:

• Usually none required, sometimes a wrench for the cable clamp bolt at the brake.

PROCEDURE:

1. Find the adjuster for your particular brake. On mountain bike brakes, it's usually on the brake lever at the point where the outer cable comes out of the lever body.

   Establish what kind of adjuster it is. On most modern road bikes, it's the type without a locknut. On older bikes it may be the type with a locknut.

2. Also find the cable quick-release, which on most road bike brakes is on the brake arm where the inner cable is clamped in. On V-brakes, it's the bent piece of metal tubing that guides the outer cable between the brake arms—to use it, squeeze the brake arms together at the top and wiggle that tube out from the bracket that holds it at the bottom. Don't do anything yet.

3. Depending on the type of adjuster:

Fig. 7.12. Pulling in the brake lever while removing the cable.

- If you're working on a bike with the adjuster without locknut, first use the quick-release to untension the cable. Then turn the adjuster in about one turn (to tighten) or out (in case you want the brake to grab later than it does now). Then tighten the quick-release again, check and repeat if necessary.
- If you're working on a bike with an adjuster with a locknut, proceed as follows:

4. Loosen the locknut by several turns, which can usually be done by hand, without the need for a tool.

5. Turn the adjusting barrel relative to the part into which it is screwed (to loosen) or out (to tighten) the tension on the cable. Loosening will open up the brake; tightening will do the opposite.

6. Holding the adjusting barrel with one hand, tighten the locknut again, then check and repeat if necessary.

7. If you run out of adjusting range, the cable has to be clamped in at a different point:

Release the cable tension with the quick-release (or unhook the cable) and then loosen the adjuster as far as possible (after unscrewing the locknut, if present).

Loosen the bolt or the nut that clamps the end of the inner cable at one of the brake arms (or, in the case of cantilever and centerpull brakes, the particular location where the main cable ends) by about one full turn.

With the needle-nose pliers, pull the cable about $3/8$ inch (1 cm) further in and tighten the bolt or the nut again.

8. Tighten the adjuster (and the locknut, if provided) about $1/4$ of the

Left: Fig. 7.13. Clamping in the cable at the V-brake.

Right: Fig. 7.14. Removing or installing a V-brake arm (follow the same procedure on a cantilever brake).

way, then tighten the quick-release and check operation of the brake—and repeat step 6.

Adjust Brake Pads

Make this correction if the brake test or any other inspection revealed that the brake pads do not lie flat and straight on the side of the rim with about $1/16$ inch (1–2 mm) clearance to the tire when the brake lever is pulled in.

Tools and equipment:

• matching wrenches

Procedure:

1. Holding the brake pad with one hand, undo the bolt or the nut that holds it to the brake arm by about one turn—just enough to allow controlled movement into the right position.

Fig. 7.15. Spreader spring holes: select to produce the desired return force.

2. While applying the brake lever so the brake pad is pushed up against the rim, twist the brake pad into the appropriate orientation and hold it firmly in place there.

3. While holding the brake pad firmly, let go of the brake lever (unless you have an assistant to do that for you) use the free hand to tighten the bolt or the nut that holds the brake pad to the brake arm.

4. Check to make sure both brake pads are properly aligned now and make any corrections necessary, then retighten.

Toeing-in note:

Preferably, the front ends (the "trailing edges") of the brake pads should touch the rim first, with the whole pad engaging only when more force is applied. This is achieved by a procedure called "toeing in," described under *Brake Squeal Compensation.*

Brake Centering

This work is required if one brake pad touches the rim before the other one, especially if it rubs on the surface of the rim while riding.

Depending on the type of brake, you may be able to find one or more small grub screws that point in sideways at the pivots. Check what happens if you tighten or loosen these screws. Adjust these screws until the brake works symmetrically, if possible. Then make sure the brake is still working properly in other ways and make any final adjustments that may be needed.

If there is no such screw, or if the desired result cannot be obtained, you may have to rotate the entire brake a little (usually the case on older caliper brakes). Do that either with a small thin wrench that fits two flat surfaces on the mounting bolt on many sidepull brakes. Otherwise, undo the mounting bolt, realign the entire brake and hold it steady there, applying force at the lever; then tighten the mounting bolt again.

On V-and cantilever brakes, the asymmetrical action may be due to uneven spring tension at the brake arms. To correct that, remove the brake arms, as described under *Overhaul Brake*, and either hook one or both of the springs into a different hole on the mounting plate (if provided) on the pivot boss—or use pliers to tension one of the springs more. Then reassemble the brake arms, check operation of the brake, and make any other adjustments that may be needed.

BRAKE SQUEAL

Sometimes, brakes seem to work alright but make a squealing noise when applied. You may have to just live with it, but it's worthwhile checking whether it can be eliminated first. That's probably possible if your brake pads are mounted with some intermediate parts between the brake arm and the pad itself. These allow you to rotate the pad in another direction as well as around the mounting bolt alone.

If the brake pads can be rotated in the other plane, adjust the pad so that the front of the pad touches the rim when there is still 2 mm ($^3/_{32}$ inch) of "air" between the pad and the rim in the back. This condition is referred to as "toed in." If this does not do the trick, also try it the other way round, the back touching the rim first (which you might call "toed out"). If still no luck, you'd probably best put it back in the position where the whole pad touches the rim at the same time.

BRAKE RUMBLE COMPENSATION

If the rumbling noises are generated when braking, and perhaps the whole bike vibrates, when you apply the brake,

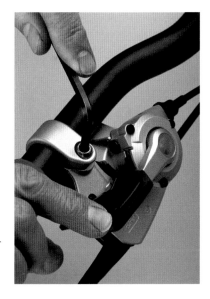

Fig. 7.16. Installing or removing a brake lever.

7

it may be a matter of a irregularly dirty wheel rim, on which the brake pad does not have a good continuous contact when you apply the brake. So check that first and clean and dry the side of the rims thoroughly.

If this does not solve the problem, it's usually because something is loose somewhere on your bike, and you'd better tighten it. First suspect is the brake itself. Check the mounting bolts of the brakes and the individual brake arms and all related pivot points. However, sometimes it's another part of the bike that's loose—most typically the headset, for which you are referred to Chapter 13.

REPLACE BRAKE CABLE

If operating the brake seems to require excessive force despite poor braking, the problem is probably due to the cable. It may be kinked, dirty or corroded, or there may be broken strands. Inspect the cable for obvious signs of damage. Re-

place it if cleaning and lubrication does not alleviate the problem. Buy a replacement cable of at least the same length, making sure it has the same type of nipple at the end where it is hooked into the brake lever.

TOOLS AND EQUIPMENT:

- wrench for inner cable clamp bolt at brake
- needle-nose pliers
- lubricant
- cloth
- cable cutters or diagonal cutters

PROCEDURE:

1. Undo the bolt or the nut that clamps in the cable at the brake.

2. Pull the brake lever and let go again while restraining the cable to loosen the cable. Catch any sections of outer cable that were used and any ferrules that went around the end of the

Fig. 7.17. Special brake lever with a fixed "drag" position latch for downhill speed control.

outer cable where it was held at anchor points.

On mountain bike brake levers, the brake cable can usually be lifted out easily once you turn the adjuster and the locknut into such an orientation that the grooves that are cut into both parts line up with a cutout in the brake mounting bracket.

3. Apply some lubricant (wax or grease on a cloth) to the new inner cable before installing it.

4. Depress the brake lever and find the place where the cable nipple is held, then insert the cable (you may need to wiggle and twist the innards of the lever a little at the point where the nipple is held to do that).

    The brake cable can usually be installed at the lever by turning the adjuster and the locknut into such an orientation that the slots cut into both parts line up with the cutout in the brake mounting bracket.

5. Route the inner cable through the various sections of outer cable and cable stops (making sure to install the ferrules at the points where the outer cable ends at the cable stops, the brake, and the lever).

6. Clamp the end of the inner cable in at the termination point on the brake while pulling it taut with the needle-nose pliers.

7. Make a provisional adjustment of the brake tension and then test the brake operation, making any final adjustments in accordance with the relevant parts of the procedure *Brake Adjustments*.

REPLACE BRAKE LEVERS

This is probably only necessary if you've had an accident with the bike. Before removing the brake lever, you may have to remove the handgrip.

7

TOOLS AND EQUIPMENT:

- wrench for lever mounting bolt
- needle-nose pliers
- wrench for brake cable clamp bolt (at the brake)

Fig. 7.18. Hydraulically-operated rim brake.

PROCEDURE:

1. Remove the brake cable, following the procedure *Replace Brake Cable.*

2. Locate the mounting bolt. If it's not externally visible, it will be accessed either from inside when you depress the brake lever (on conventional brake levers) or from under the rubber brake hood (on most integrated brake/shift levers). Loosen the bolt far enough to slide (and usually wiggle) the lever off to the end of the handlebars.

3. Loosen the bolt on the replacement lever just far enough to allow it to slide over the handlebars (but try not to take it out all the way, because it can be very hard to get the various parts of the mounting clamp together once the bolt is out).

4. Slide the lever into position and orient it so that it can be comfortably

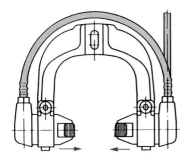

Fig. 7.19. Hydraulic rim brake operating diagram.

reached while riding the bike. (If necessary, use the lever on the opposite side of the handlebars as a guide regarding the angle and the mounting position.)

5. Tighten the mounting bolt fully, making sure the lever stays in the correct position and orientation.

6. Reinstall the cable as described under Replace Brake Cable, and test operation of the brake, making any adjustments that may be necessary as described under *Brake Adjustments.*

OVERHAUL BRAKE

1. Untension the quick-release or unhook the cable at the brake.

2. Remove the brake cable clamping bolt.

3. Remove the bolts with which the brake arms are installed on their pivots, then also remove the brake pads from the brake arms.

4. Remove all other components (including springs, bushings, and washers).

5. Clean and inspect the condition of all parts and replace anything damaged.

6. Slightly lubricate all parts and apply wax to the exterior surfaces, then re-

assemble all parts on the brake assembly (on caliper brakes) or the pivots (on V-brakes or cantilever brakes).

On some cantilever brakes and V-brakes, there is a choice of three holes to insert the end of the spring

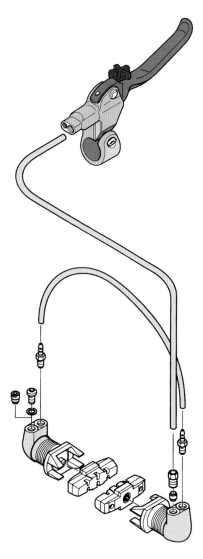

at each pivot, depending on the spring tension. First choose the middle hole; if after assembly the brake turns out not to be centered and no amount of adjusting will cure it, undo the brake pivot bolt again, insert the spring in one of the other holes (depending on whether this was the one with too much or the one with too little tension), and reinstall the brake arm.

7. Reattach the cable and adjust it loosely, then tension the quick-release (caliper brake) or attach the outer cable (V-brake or cantilever brake) and make the final adjustment.

8. Test operation of the brake and make any adjustments necessary.

7

Right: Fig. 7.22. On the hydraulic brake lever, check the connection between the lever's reservoir and the hydraulic tube for damage or leaks.

Above: Fig. 9.20. Hydraulic rim brake system overview diagram.

HYDRAULIC RIM BRAKES

Although hydraulic systems are common with disk brakes, Magura also makes an excellent hydraulically operated rim brake. The illustrations on these pages give an overview of relevant information. For a more thorough treatment of hydraulic controls, please refer to the instructions in Chapter 8.

7.21. Installing hydraulic rim brake lever.

8

Disk Brake Maintenance

First used only on downhill mountain bikes, disk brakes have now become common on many types of high-end bikes. This chapter deals with their installation and basic maintenance, including the issues relating to hydraulic operation.

Operating Principle

In essence, a disk brake works like a regular rim brake, except that the rim is replaced by a flat circular disk attached to the wheel hub. A pair of brake pads are held in a set of (usually hydraulically operated) calipers mounted on a frame tube, so that they can clamp down on the rotating disk to slow it down. The function of the counter lever that's part of all other hub brakes, is taken over by a set of two attachment lugs that hold the brake caliper unit to the fork or the rear stays.

Disk brakes can be operated two ways: either by means of cables like most other hand-operated brakes or via a hydraulic system similar to what's used on cars and motorcycles. In the latter case, the (special) brake lever incorporates a hydraulic oil reservoir, and there'll be another reservoir at the cali-

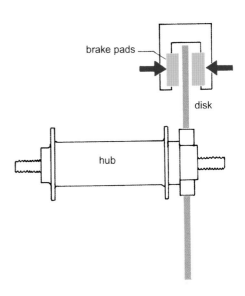

Fig. 8.1. Disk brake operation diagram.

per unit. The two are connected by means of hydraulic tubing.

BRAKE TEST

To test whether a disk brake works properly, follow the following procedure:

1. First check to make sure all components of the system (brake, lever, and tubing) are firmly attached and there's no sign of leakage of hydrau-

lic liquid (or, in the case of cable-operation, no frayed or kinked cables.

2. Riding slowly, it should be possible to apply the front brake forcefully enough for the rear wheel to start lifting off the ground. Then immediately let go of that brake.

3. For the rear brake, it should be possible to make the wheel skid on smooth, dry pavement.
   If the brake does not perform adequately, the most common cause is air in the hydraulic system. Follow the bleeding instructions given under *Hydraulic System Maintenance* to correct this problem.

   Make sure the brake levers are mounted close enough to the center of the handlebars to allow you to grip the end of the lever. You can apply more force there.

Above: Fig. 8.2. Manufacturer's diagram of a typical hydraulic disk brake system (Magura).

Right: Fig. 8.3. Typical front-wheel disk brake.

DISK CHECK AND MAINTENANCE

The brake disk is attached to the (special) hub by means of shallow-headed Allen bolts or Torx bolts (similar to Allen bolts but with a star-shaped recess instead of hexagonal ones). Use a fitting Allen or Torx wrench to make sure they are properly tightened.

Keep hydraulic liquid and other oils away from the disk, and clean any oil, dirt, or brake pad deposits with rubbing alcohol.

If the disk drags on the calipers, it's not corrected by anything you do to the disk but by moving the calipers in or out a little (see below).

BRAKE CLEANING AND MAINTENANCE

TOOLS AND EQUIPMENT

• clean rag
• isopropyl alcohol
• wrenches

PROCEDURE

1. Check for leaks at the connections of the hydraulic tube at the brake lever and at the brake, as well as at the brake unit itself. If there are any signs of leaking, take the bike to a

Above: Fig. 8.4. Checking attachment bolts of disk brake caliper unit. This illustration depicts the standard caliper attachment to the side of the fork's slider tube, as opposed to the type shown in Fig. 8.7.

Right: Fig. 8.5. Whenever the wheel is removed, place the protector between the pads.

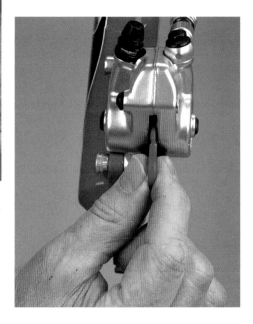

8

bike mechanic to deal with the problem, since the work involved is not suitable for the home mechanic.

2. Clean all parts with a clean cloth and cleaning alcohol.

3. Check the firmness of the nuts that hold the hydraulic tube connectors at the brake lever and at the brake unit, tightening only to the level prescribed by the manufacturer (don't overtighten).

4. Check the bolts holding the disk to the wheel and tighten only to the torque level prescribed by the manufacturer (don't overtighten).

5. Clean both sides of the disk with a clean cloth and isopropyl alcohol. (If the inside of the disk can not be cleaned properly this way, remove the disk to clean it and reinstall it, bolting it down firmly.

6. Remove the brake pads in accordance with the preceding instruction *Replace Brake Pads*, and inspect their condition, replacing them if worn below 2 mm in thickness or if they are grease-stained.

7. Adjust the brake as described under *Brake Adjustment*.

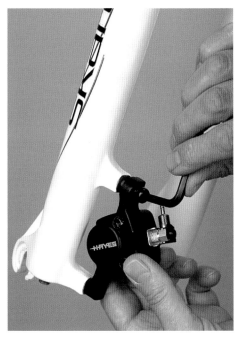

Left: Fig. 8.6. The disk is attached to the hub's mounting flange with 5 or 6 Torx screws.

Above: Fig. 8.7. Attaching caliper to an Answer/Manitou-type mounting, i.e., to the back of the fork.

BRAKE CALIPER MAINTENANCE

The calipers are attached to standardized bosses attached to the frame at the rear dropout and to the back of the front fork. They're held in place with 6 mm Allen bolts, and they too must be kept firmly tightened.

Never apply the brake lever when the wheel (with the disk) is not in the bike. This would make the brake pads bind together, making it hard to separate them. Always insert the plastic protector plate that comes with the brake unit.

Clean the pads with a piece of emery cloth about once a month or whenever the brakes squeal.

The disk should run exactly in the middle between the brake pads. There is an adjusting knobs on one side of the calipers, which can be turned in or out to adjust the pad location until they are both equally far from the disk. Any additional adjustments are done by adding or removing spacers around the mounting bolts, between the brake unit and the lugs on the frame.

There are two mounting standards, as illustrated in Fig. 8.4 and 8.7 and referred to as "standard" and "Answer/Manitou" respectively. Usually, brakes come with an adaptor to convert from one standard to the other.

In general, I do not recommend installing disk brakes on a bike that was originally equipped without them, because it can be very difficult to make the whole assembly of frame, brake, wheel, and disk aligned properly. Stick with whatever type of brakes your bike came with, and if it came with disk brakes, don't try to replace them by disk brakes of a different make or model.

8

Left: Fig. 8.8. Attaching bleeding tube to caliper.

Above: Fig. 8.9. Adjust the reservoir cap to leave no air bubble on top.

HYDRAULIC SYSTEM MAINTENANCE

If the brakes feel "spongy," you'll have to bleed the system, i.e., let air bubbles out. At least once a year, you should flush all the oil out and replace it with fresh oil.

There are two different types of hydraulic liquid in use for hydraulic brakes DOT No. 4 and hydraulic oil. Both are available in automotive supply stores more cheaply than in a bike shop (but be careful not to ruin the seals by using the wrong type for the make and model installed on your bike).

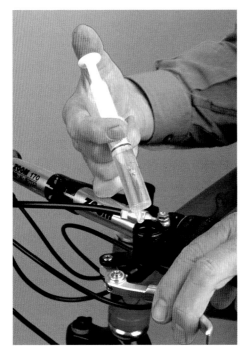

Fig. 8.10. Filling oil into the lever reservoir using a plastic syringe.

TOOLS AND EQUIPMENT:

- latex gloves
- 12 in (30 cm) of ⅛ in. flexible plastic tubing
- small plastic syringe
- small plastic bottle
- only if replenishing: hydraulic liquid of the specified type
- empty jam jar
- any tools required to open reservoir at brake lever

NOTE:

Since the fluid used is toxic, always wear latex gloves when doing this work, and dispose of all materials (don't reuse those latex gloves).

PROCEDURE

1. Clamp the bike in the repair stand so that the bake lever is as high as possible and the brake unit as low as possible. Turn the brake lever so that the reservoir cover is horizontal.

2. Remove the screws to open up the reservoir at the brake lever.

3. Attach the tube to the bleed nipple at the brake unit holding the tube pointing straight up, but curved down at the top to drain into the jam jar. Then open the bleed nipple about ¼ turn.

4. Fill the syringe with brake fluid and start filling it into the reservoir at the lever while gently pumping the lever repeatedly.

5. Watch the oil being pushed through the bleed tube and keep filling until no air bubbles come through.

6. Close the bleed nipple and the reservoir at the lever.

7. Test operation of the brakes and if necessary repeat until the brake action is firm.

Replace Brake Pads

Tools and equipment:

- needle-nose pliers
- replacement split pins, if applicable

Removal instructions:

1. Find the clip or the split pins that hold the brake pads in place on the brake unit.

2. If there are split pins, straighten out their ends with the needle-nose pliers and pull out the pins, or just pull out the clip.

3. Lift and pull out the metal plates that hold the pads.

Installation procedure:

1. Inspect the condition of the pads, and replace them with identical units if they are worn to less than 2 mm thickness or if there are signs of grease on the surface.

2. Push the far end in pointing in toward the housing on the applicable side and click the entire unit into position.

3. Reinsert the clip or insert the new split pins and bend their ends out so they stay in place.

8

Fig. 8.11. Replacing a brake pad on a disk brake caliper.

4. Check operation of the brake and make any adjustments that may be necessary.

REPLACE DISK

TOOLS AND EQUIPMENT

- wrenches to match attachment bolts (either Allen wrench or torx wrench)

1. Use only the same size disk from the same manufacturer as the original as replacement.

2. Remove the wheel from the bike.

3. Firmly holding the wheel clamped in, undo the attachment bolts, pushing down on the bolts firmly to make sure the tool does not slip out of the shallow recesses in the bolts.

4. Remove the disk.

5. Clean all parts that are now accessible, including the disk per the instruction *Disk Brake Cleaning and Maintenance*.

6. Install the disk, by installing the bolts only loosely at first.

7. Tighten the bolts in the following sequence:
   - Pick which bolt you will tighten first, and bolt it down with modest hand force.
   - Work around tightening every second bolt, i.e., always skipping one bolt. Since there are 5 bolts, you will have tightened each one after working around twice this way.

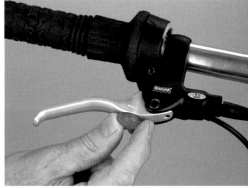

Above: Fig. 8.12. Close-up of disk and matching mounting flange on the hub.

Right: Fig. 8.13. Hydraulic brake lever.

• Now work around twice more tightening to the prescribed torque level.

8. Reinsert the wheel, check operation of the brake, and make any adjustments that may be necessary.

HYDRAULIC BRAKE LEVERS

Most hydraulic levers are attached the same way as regular cable-operated levers. When replacing the handlebars, take care not to damage the connection between the hydraulic tube and the lever. The amount of lever travel can be adjusted by means of a set screw on the lever.

CABLE-OPERATED DISK BRAKES

Lower-end disk brakes are usually cable-operated, and there's really nothing wrong with that, because they're a lot easier to fix and maintain than hydraulic systems. For work involving cables and the matching levers, refer to the appropriate sections in Chapter 7.

Finally, it's possible to combine cable and hydraulic operation. This isn't something you'll frequently encounter though.

Fig. 8.14. Adjusting a cable-operated disk brake at the rear caliper.

8

9 DERAILLEUR GEAR MAINTENANCE

All mountain bikes are equipped with derailleur gearing, and this chapter addresses maintenance of these systems. The derailleur system consists of a rear derailleur and a front derailleur, controlled by means of shifters to which the derailleurs are connected by means of gear control cables.

The rear derailleur selects one of usually 9 cogs on the rear freewheel with different numbers of teeth, and the front derailleur selects one of three chainrings in the front.

Mountain bikes are either shifted by means of a rotating twist grip or by means of shift levers mounted under the handlebars, just inboard from the brake levers.

Fig. 9.1.
Derailleur
gearing system
on a typical
mountain bike.

Think of derailleur gearing as a system, because if there is a problem, it may be due to any of a number of factors ranging from the derailleur mechanism to the cable to the shifter—in fact, even the chain or the cogs and chainrings may be at fault. Keep that in mind when troubleshooting for gearing problems. None of the components require much in the way of maintenance other than keeping them clean and occasional adjusting.

The chainrings are described in Chapter 10; the other components of the gearing system will be covered here.

As for terminology, this text adheres to the manufacturers' preferred nomenclature. In the UK, the front derailleur is often called a "changer," while the rear derailleur is often referred to as a "mech," short for mechanism.

THE REAR DERAILLEUR

Take a look at the rear derailleur. It consists of a metal cage with two little wheels, or pulleys, over which the chain is guided, and a spring-tensioned parallelogram mechanism that moves the cage sideways to line up with the different cogs on the freewheel at the rear wheel hub. Note the various adjusting

9

Right: Fig. 9.2. Derailleur system in the highest gear: Front derailleur on the largest chainring, rear derailleur on the smallest cog.

Left: Fig. 9.3. Derailleur system in the lowest gear: smallest chainring in front, largest cog in back.

9

screws sticking out at different points and the adjusting barrel for the cable tension.

The most common problems at the rear derailleur are over- or undershifting and failure to index properly at the gear selected. Both these problems can usu-

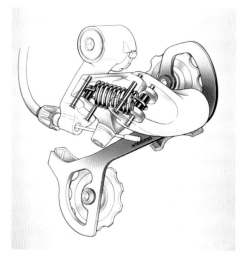

ally be overcome with simple adjustments.

- overshifting occurs when the chain is shifted too far in the highest or the lowest gear, getting caught between the smallest cog and the frame or between the biggest cog and the wheel respectively.
- undershifting occurs when the chain doesn't get shifted far enough at the smallest or the biggest cog, so the corresponding gear cannot be engaged.
- Failure to index properly occurs when the chain doesn't line up with the cog, so the gear does not engage correctly—either skipping gears or running in gear with a scraping noise. The most common problem, improper indexing, is adjusted easily with the cable adjusting barrel on the derailleur.

Above: Fig. 9.4. Manufacturer's cut-away diagram of a rear derailleur (Shimano).

Left: Fig. 9.5. Rear derailleur in the highest gear: the chain engaging the smallest cog.

Right: Fig. 9.6. Rear derailleur in low gear, the chain engaging the largest cog.

ADJUST REAR DERAILLEUR

When the gears do not engage properly, it's a good idea to first make sure the cable is in good condition (and replace it if it isn't). Then proceed as follows to adjust:

TOOLS AND EQUIPMENT:

• Usually none required (sometimes a wrench to fit the cable clamp bolt)

PROCEDURE:

1. Place the bike in an intermediate gear.

2. Locate the adjusting mechanism at the point where the control cable enters the derailleur.

3. Turn the adjuster out in ½-turn increments and try shifting through the entire range of gears, while turning the cranks with the wheel lifted off the ground. Note whether the problem gets better or worse.
   • If the problem gets better, continue adjusting in small increments until it indexes properly.
   • If the problem gets worse, turn the adjuster in the opposite direction until the derailleur indexes properly.

4. If you can't turn the adjuster in or out far enough. Use the additional adjuster at the shifter that may be present on bikes with flat handlebars. Select the highest gear, i.e., the smallest cog and, using the needle-nose pliers to pull the cable taut, clamp it in at a different point.

Left: Fig. 9.7. Adjusting the cable tension for the gears on the derailleur.

Right: Fig. 9.8. Rear derailleur in the process of shifting the chain between cogs.

5. If the highest or lowest gear cannot be reached properly, or the chain shifts beyond the gear, refer to *Rear Derailleur Over-and undershift Adjustment.*

ANGLE ADJUSTMENT NOTE:

• On most modern derailleurs, there is a separate adjustment screw near the derailleur mounting point, to adjust the limiting angle of the derailleur cage relative to the horizontal plane. You may try adjusting this one way or the other, bringing the chain and the upper pulley (called "jockey pulley") closer to, or farther from, the cogs.

REAR DERAILLEUR OVER-AND UNDER-SHIFT ADJUSTMENT

This problem is particularly prevalent after the rear wheel or the cogs on the rear wheel have been replaced. How-

ever, it can also be due to either normal wear or damage in an accident (in which case you should first check for, and correct, any damage).

TOOLS AND EQUIPMENT:

• small screwdriver

PROCEDURE:

1. Find the two small adjusting screws that limit the sideways travel of the derailleur cage. Usually, one is marked "H" for high, limiting travel toward the high gear (outside, smallest cog), the other one "L" for low, limiting travel toward the low gear (inside, biggest cog).
    • If they're not marked, place the bike in the highest or the lowest gear (smallest or biggest cog in the rear) and establish which is which by turning one of them in (clockwise) to find out whether that results in less movement to the outside (that would be "H") or the inside ("L").

Above: Fig. 9.9. Adjusting the range limit screws on the rear derailleur.

Right: Fig. 9.10. Adjusting the "angle of dangle" setting screw on the rear derailleur.

2. Depending on the problem, turn the relevant adjusting screw in or out in ½-turn increments:

• Turn the "H" screw in to compensate for overshifting at the high gear (i.e., the chain was shifted beyond the smallest cog), or out to compensate for undershifting at the high end (i.e., the chain did not quite reach that smallest cog).

• Turn the "L" screw in to compensate for overshifting at the low gear (i.e., the chain was shifted beyond the largest cog), or out to compensate for undershifting at the low end (i.e., the chain did not quite reach that largest cog).

3. Lift the wheel off the ground and turn the crank, shifting into all the gears, and fine-tune the adjustment until it works the way it should.

Also see the *Angle adjustment note* on the preceding page.

REAR DERAILLEUR OVERHAUL

Before starting with this work, you may want to undo the cable attachment at the derailleur—however, then you'll have to readjust the system afterwards. Usually, the work can be done with the derailleur still attached to its cable.

TOOLS AND EQUIPMENT:

• Allen wrenches (or regular wrenches for older models)
• cloths
• solvent and lubricant

9

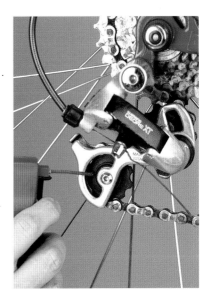

Left: Fig. 9.11. Adjusting the range limit screw on the front derailleur.

Right: Fig. 9.12. Lubricating the derailleur pulley bearings. But clean them thoroughly before you lubricate them.

PROCEDURE:

1. Remove the bolt that holds the lower pulley.

2. Remove the lower pulley (the tension wheel); now the chain can be removed from the derailleur cage.

3. Also remove the other pulley (the jockey wheel).

4. Clean, inspect, and lubricate all parts. Replace the pulleys if they can't be made to turn freely.

5. Reinstall the jockey wheel.

6. Put the chain back in the cage.

7. Install the tension wheel.

8. Check operation and make any adjustments necessary per the preceding procedures.

REPLACE REAR DERAILLEUR

The rear derailleur is held by means of an Allen mounting bolt, which attaches it to an extension of the right-hand dropout called "derailleur eye." On cheap bikes, it may be attached to a separate mounting plate held between the hub and the dropout. Make sure the new derailleur is designed for the particular range of cogs on your wheel. To handle big gearing steps, you need a wide-range derailleur, characterized by a big cage—with the pulleys far apart.

Left: Fig. 9.13. Lubricating the rear derailleur parallelogram pivots.

Right: Fig. 9.14. Removal or installation of rear derailleur pulley.

Tools and equipment

- Allen wrenches, sometimes (for older derailleurs), just one Allen wrench and a 7 mm open-ended or box wrench.

Removal procedure:

1. Put the rear derailleur in the highest gear (smallest cog) and remove the cable, following the procedure for cable replacement.

2. Remove the jockey pulley to free the chain (alternately, you can disconnect the chain, following the procedure in Chapter 11).

3. Remove the mounting bolt, and take the derailleur off the bike.

Installation procedure:

1. Install the mounting bolt, while pushing the derailleur up against the spring tension so that it clears the derailleur eye (or the mounting plate).

2. If necessary, remove the tension wheel, then slide the chain in, and reinstall the tension wheel.

3. Attach the cable.

4. Make any adjustments that may be necessary, following the procedures above.

9

Adjust Front Derailleur

When the gears do not engage properly in the front, first make sure the cable is

Left: Fig. 9.15. Installing rear derailleur pulley.

Above: Fig. 9.16. Tightening, installing, or removing rear derailleur.

in good condition (and replace it if it isn't). Then proceed to adjust.

- Usually none required (sometimes a wrench to fit the cable clamp bolt)

PROCEDURE:

1. Select the gear that combines the middle chainring with an intermediate cog.

2. Locate the adjusting mechanism at the point where the control cable enters the derailleur.

3. Turn the adjuster out in ½-turn increments, and try shifting through the entire range of gears, turning the cranks with the wheel lifted off the ground. Note whether the problem gets better or worse.
   - If the problem gets better, continue adjusting in ½-turn increments until the derailleur indexes properly.
   - If the problem gets worse, turn the adjuster in the opposite direction until the derailleur indexes properly.

4. If there is not enough adjustment to solve the problem:
   Use the additional adjuster at the shifter that may be present on bikes with flat handlebars.
   If still no luck, elect the highest gear, i.e., the largest chainring, then clamp the cable in at a different point with the wrench, using the needle-nose pliers to pull the cable taut.

5. If the highest or lowest gear cannot be reached properly, or the chain

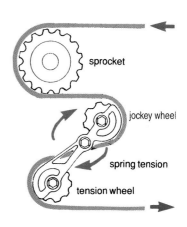

Left: Fig. 9.17. Replacing rear derailleur cable.

Right: Fig. 9.18. Chain routing at rear derailleur.

shifts beyond the gear, refer to *Over- and Undershift Adjustment* below.

Front Derailleur Over-and Under-shift Adjustment

When this problem occurs at the front derailleur, the chain gets stuck beyond the small or the big chainring (over-shift), or it can't be shifted onto one of the chainrings (undershift). It may either be due to normal wear or damage in an accident (in which case you should first check for, and correct, any damage).

Tools and equipment:

*   small screwdriver

Procedure:

1. Find the two small adjusting screws on top, which limit the sideways travel of the front derailleur cage.

Usually, one is marked "H" for high, limiting travel toward the high gear (outside, large chainring), the other one "L" for low, limiting travel toward the low gear (inside, small chainring). If they're not marked, establish which is which by turning one of them in (clockwise) to find out whether that results in less movement to the inside (that would be "L") or the outside (that would be "H").

2. Depending on the problem, turn the relevant adjusting screw in or out in $\frac{1}{2}$-turn increments:
    *   Turn the "H" screw in to compensate for overshifting at the high gear (i.e., the chain was shifted beyond the largest chainring), or out to compensate for undershifting at the high end (i.e., the chain did not quite reach that largest chainring).

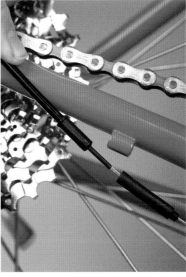

Above: Fig. 9.19. Installation of rear derailleur

Right: Fig. 9.20. Cable routing for rear derailleur.

• Turn the "L" screw in to compensate for overshifting at the low gear (i.e., the chain was shifted beyond the smallest chainring), or out to compensate for undershifting at the low end (i.e., the chain did not quite reach that smallest chainring).

3. Lift the wheel off the ground and turn the crank, shifting into all the gears, and fine-tune the adjustment until it works the way it should.

REPLACE DERAILLEUR CABLE

Replace the cable if it is hard to move, either because it is corroded or damaged, e.g., is pinched, kinked, or frayed. Whether for the front or the rear derailleur, the procedure is the same. If it's an indexed derailleur, buy a cable for the particular derailleur on your bike (yes, nowadays they're quite specific); if not, just make sure it's a cable with the right type of nipple (check at the shifter what shape and size it has). Before you start, put the bike in the gear that engages the smallest cog in the rear or the smallest chainring in the front.

TOOLS AND EQUIPMENT:

• wrench for cable clamp at derailleur
• needle-nose pliers
• cable cutters
• sometimes diagonal cutters
• cloth and lubricant (preferably wax)

PROCEDURE:

1. Undo the cable clamp bolt at the derailleur.

Left: Fig. 9.21. Adjusting the front derailleur.

Above: Fig. 9.22. Routing of "downpull" type cable at front derailleur. Regular operation is "uppull" with the cable coming from above.

2. At the shifter, pull the outer cable back a little and then push the inner cable in toward the shifter to expose the nipple at the shifter and enough cable to reach that point with the pliers.

3. Pull the cable out, first with the pliers, then by hand, catching the various sections of outer cable at the shifter and (on a rear derailleur) at the derailleur.

4. Make sure the new cable and the outer cable sections are of the same type and length as the original. Then apply some lubricant to the inner cable.

5. Starting at the shifter, install the inner cable through the shifter, the outer cable sections, over or through any guides on the frame, and into the derailleur itself.

6. Clamp the cable end provisionally (i.e., not too tight yet).

7. Try the gears, turning the cranks with the wheel lifted off the ground, and adjust the cable (both with the adjuster and with the cable clamp bolt) until all gears work properly— refer to the preceding procedures *Adjust Rear Derailleur* and *Adjust Front Derailleur*.

REPLACE FRONT DERAILLEUR

Front derailleurs are either mounted with a clamp that fits around the seat tube or directly on a tab that's welded to the seat tube. Either way, they'll be held

9

Left: Fig. 9.23. Installation of cable at front derailleur.

Above: Fig. 9.24. Tightening, installing, or removing front derailleur.

with an Allen bolt on modern bikes, while on older bikes it may be a conventional hexagonal-head bolt and nut.

TOOLS AND EQUIPMENT:

- Allen wrenches (or whatever kind of wrenches fit)
- screwdriver to open up the derailleur cage to remove the chain

REMOVAL PROCEDURE:

1. Remove the little screw that holds the two sides of the derailleur cage together so you can remove the chain (or, if it cannot easily be opened, disconnect the chain, following the instructions in Chapter 11).

2. Undo the cable.

3. Remove the mounting bolt and remove the derailleur.

INSTALLATION PROCEDURE:

1. Place the mounting bolt on the derailleur eye or the mounting plate and thread it in about 1½ turns by hand.

2. Swivel the derailleur back against the spring tension until it passes the prong on the derailleur eye or the mounting plate; then screw the bolt in further with the wrench.

3. Open up the cage and remove the jockey pulley.

4. Feed the chain through and reinstall the jockey pulley, holding back the derailleur cage against its spring tension.

5. Place the chain on the appropriate cog and chainring.

Above: Fig. 9.25. Shifter with position indicator.

Right: Fig. 9.26. Installing, removing, or tightening twist-grip type shifter.

6. Attach the cable.

7. Check operation of the gears and make any adjustments necessary, following the procedure above.

Shifter Maintenance

There's not much you can do on modern integrated shifters: they either work or they have to be replaced in their entirety. If your bike is equipped with separately mounted shifters, you can simply take them apart and see whether there's something damaged or, more typically, loose, dirty, or corroded. Fix what you find to be wrong and tighten the bolt that holds everything together when done. Adjust the relevant derailleur after such work, and chances are you've taken care of the problem. If not, you'll just have to replace the entire shifter.

Freewheel and Cogs

The rear wheel cogs are mounted on a freewheel mechanism, which contains a kind of ratcheting system to turn forward when driven by the rider without forcing the rider to pedal forward all the time.

The freewheel is either integrated into a portion of the hub (in the case of the modern so-called cassette hub) or in a separate unit that is screwed on to the hub (in the case of the older freewheel block). The various cogs are either screwed on or held on splines and held together with a screwed-on item (either a separate lock ring or the smallest cog).

At least once a year, clean the cogs—and the spaces between them. To clean between the cogs, use a thin cloth folded into a narrow strip, stretched between both hands, going back and forth all around (it's easiest with the wheel re-

9

Left: Fig. 9.27. Lubricating inside a cassette using a special lubricating tool.

Right: Fig. 9.28. Cleaning between the cogs.

moved off the bike). If dirt doesn't come off, soak the cloth in a mixture of solvent and 5–10% mineral oil.

Individual cogs can be replaced by first removing the last, screwed-on item. This is done with a special tool—buy the appropriate tool for the type of freewheel on your bike if you want to do this work yourself. Especially on modern cassette hubs, the choice of cogs is rather limited, in that they come in sets, and usually it will not be possible to pick different sequences of cogs, as can be done with the old-fashioned screwed-on freewheel block.

When replacing an entire cassette—or some of the cogs on a cassette—make sure they are compatible. I also suggest replacing the chain at that time, ascer-taining at the bike shop that it is suitable for the particular cassette.

One reason you might want to replace one or more of the cogs would be in case of wear, when the chain starts to skip. At that point, you should replace both the cog in question (usually the smallest one) and the chain, because the old, "stretched" chain would not fit the tooth pattern on the new cog.

The freewheel body can be lubricated with thick mineral oil (SAE 60) inserted in the visible gap between moving parts inside.

If the freewheel mechanism fails or becomes either too loose or too rough, it can be replaced. The method depends on whether it's an old-fashioned screwed-on type or the modern cassette type.

The screwed-on type is removed with a special freewheel tool: Remove the wheel, hold the tool loosely with the wheel's quick-release skewer, then un-

Above: Fig. 9.29. Disassembling a freewheel cassette.

Right: Fig. 9.30. Freewheel cassette with cogs removed.

screw it, using a large wrench, holding the wheel firmly (loosen the quick-release thumb nut as needed along the way). The cassette freewheel can be removed with a 10 mm Allen wrench as shown in Fig. 9.33. If it's a screwed-on type, clean and lubricate the screw thread, and screw the new freewheel on by hand.

To remove a cassette type freewheel, first remove the cogs per the instructions below. Then remove the hub axle, disassembling it from the opposite side. You now have access to a hollow internal 10 mm Allen bolt, removed or installed per Fig. 9.33.

When a spoke on the chain side of the rear wheel breaks, you have to remove the freewheel (in the case of a screwed-on freewheel block) or the cogs

(in the case of a cassette hub). This is probably the most common reason to remove these items.

ADAPT GEAR RANGE

If the gears on your bike are not high enough or, more typically, not low enough, you can change that by replacing chainrings or cogs with bigger or smaller ones. To achieve a higher top gear, you could exchange either the smallest cog with a smaller one or the largest chainring with a larger one. To achieve a lower low gear, replace either

Left: Fig. 9.31. Disassembling screwed-on cogs from freewheel cassette.

Above: Fig. 9.32. Removing cogs from a screwed-on freewheel.

the biggest cog by a bigger one or the smallest chainring by a smaller one.

That's the theory. In practice, these days, cogs and chainrings usually come "prepackaged" in certain combinations, and it may be hard or impossible to find a single replacement cog or chainring to match your needs. Find out at the bike shop which combinations are available to satisfy your needs and exchange them accordingly—whether individually or as set of several matching ones.

Fig. 9.33. Removing freewheel cassette from hub.

To exchange chainrings, first select a low gear, and lift the chain off the chainring. Then undo the little bolts that hold the chainrings to the right-hand crank. Install the new chainring(s) with the same bolts and replace the chain.

To exchange cogs, first remove the rear wheel. Then either unscrew the smallest cog that holds the rest together on a cassette hub, or use the chain whip to separate the cogs on a screwed-on freewheel. Put the new cog(s) in place and reinstall the wheel. If you installed larger cogs or chainrings, you may need a wide-range derailleur and a longer chain to accommodate them.

10

CRANKSET MAINTENANCE

T he crankset, or chain-set, as it is called in Britain, consists of the bottom bracket (bearings and spindle), the cranks, or crank arms, and the chainrings that are connected to the right-hand crank.

The crankset is part of the bicycle's overall transmission system, or drivetrain—together with the pedals, the chain, and the components of the gearing system. These other items will all be covered separately in subsequent chapters.

THE CRANKS

All modern mountain bikes come equipped with what is referred to as a cotterless crankset. The cranks themselves are made of aluminum alloy—nice and light, but it does mean that the screw thread is quite sensitive and must be treated carefully.

On these, the ends of the bottom bracket spindle are either tapered in a square pattern or splined. The crank has a correspondingly patterned recess on

the inside (i.e., the side facing the bike's frame).

There are two types: with solid spindle and with hollow spindle. On the former, both cranks are held on to the

Fig. 10.1. Modern hollow-spindle crankset with externally mounted bearings and split crank attachment.

spindle by means of a bolt (or sometimes a nut), which sits in a larger threaded cylindrical crank recess facing out, and on older models there's a dustcap covering the recess.

On hollow-spindle models, such as Shimano's Hollowtech crankset, the right-side crank is permanently attached to the (hollow) spindle, while the left-side crank is split at the end and clamped around the splined spindle by means of two Allen bolts.

The screw thread in the cylindrical recess allows removal of the cranks with a special matching tool, although some high-end cranksets may have a clever "one-key-release" system on which the attachment bolt also serves as a crank puller (for these, you'll only require an 8 mm Allen wrench).

The right-hand crank has either a "spider" to which the chainrings are attached at 4 or 5 points by means of small bolts and nuts.

At the end opposite the one where the crank is installed on the bottom bracket spindle, there is a hole with

screw thread for the pedal. The one on the right has regular right-hand screw thread, while the one on the left has left-hand screw thread (that's so the left pedal doesn't work loose as you pedal the bike).

TIGHTEN CRANK

Do this work in conjunction with the monthly inspection, and whenever you hear or feel creaking or other signs of looseness in the connection between the crank and the bottom bracket. For the recent crop of hollow bottom bracket spindle cranksets, see the *Hollowtech note* at the end of this section. For all other types, proceed as follows:

TOOLS AND EQUIPMENT:

• wrench part of crank tool or specific crank bolt wrench (for some low-end and older mountain bikes) or Allen wrench (for most modern high-end mountain bikes)

Left: Fig. 10.2. Conventional square tapered crank attachment.

Right: Fig. 10.3. Hollow splined crank attachment with bolted crank attachment.

10

- tool to fit dust cap (depending on the model, either an Allen wrench, a pin wrench, a screwdriver, or a coin)
- for Hollowtech cranks: 5 mm Allen wrench

PROCEDURE FOR BIKES WITH LARGE EXPOSED ALLEN BOLT

This type is found on most modern mountain bikes:

1. Tighten the Allen bolt with the 8 mm Allen wrench, while holding the crank firmly for leverage.

2. Also tighten the other crank, even if it did not seem loose.

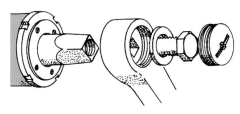

Above: Fig. 10.4. Assembly diagram of cotterless crank connection.

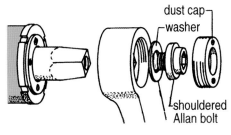

dust cap
washer
shouldered
Allan bolt

Fig. 10.5. Assembly diagram of one-key cotterless crank connection.

PROCEDURE FOR BIKES WITH SEPARATE METAL DUST CAP:

1. On older models, remove the dust cap from the threaded recess in the crank.

2. Using the wrench part of the crank tool (or a specific crank bolt wrench), tighten the bolt with the Allen wrench, while holding the crank firmly for leverage.

3. Reinstall the dust cap if applicable.

HOLLOWTECH NOTE:

On these, the right-hand crank arm with the chainrings is permanently attached to the (hollow) spindle. Only the left-hand crank has to be tightened. It is split at the end and clamped around the splined, hollow spindle with two Allen

Right: Fig. 10.6. Removing a dustcap with two recesses. Other models have either a screwdriver slot or an Allen wrench fitting.

10

bolts, one on each side. Keep these equally tightened, with moderate hand force.

REMOVE AND INSTALL CRANK

Do this work to gain access to the bottom bracket itself, e.g., for bearing overhaul, or to replace the crank, e.g., if it is bent or damaged. Also here, see the *Hollowtech note* at the end for modern hollow spindle cranksets.

TOOLS AND EQUIPMENT:

- crank tool (both the puller part and the crank bolt wrench part) and second wrench, or just an 8 mm Allen wrench (depending on the crank bolt type)

- for Hollowtech cranks: 5 mm Allen wrench

PROCEDURE:

1. Remove the dust cap and then the bolt—or the Allen bolt with a black plastic ring around it, or just loosen the Allen bolt (on splined-spindle models, which you'll recognize by the fact that there is a metal cap with two little round recesses around the 8 mm Allen bolt).

   • If the bolt or the nut comes out (non-splined-spindle models), remove any washer that may be present (very important: if you forget this step, you won't be able to pull the crank off—and ruin the screw thread in the crank).

   • On splined spindle models, just keep turning the bolt loose (which after the first one or two turns be-

Left: Fig. 10.7. Tightening or loosening a crank attachment bolt.

Right: Fig. 10.8. Using Allen wrench to tighten or loosen a one-key crank attachment bolt.

10

comes much harder to do—but persevere anyway), and it will pull the crank off the spindle.

2. On models requiring use of the crank extractor tool, make sure there is no washer left in the recess and the puller is fully retracted (i.e., the central threaded part does not project); then screw it into the threaded recess in the crank as far as possible, using the wrench.

3. Holding the outer part of the crank extractor tool with one wrench, screw in the central part with the other one.

4. The crank will be pulled off this way; then unscrew the tool from the crank.

INSTALLATION PROCEDURE:

1. Clean and inspect, and if necessary, replace parts; then apply a thin layer of grease (or preferably anti-seize lubricant) on the matching flat or splined surfaces of the bottom bracket spindle and the crank.

2. Place the crank on the bottom bracket spindle, making sure it's 180 degrees offset from the other crank,

10

Left: Fig. 10.9. The crank attachment bolt removed on a square-spindle crankset.

Above Fig. 10.10. Using crank tool to extract crank.

and push it on by hand as far as possible.

3. On non-splined-spindle models, install the washer, then the bolt, and tighten the bolt firmly, using the crank for leverage.

4. Tighten the bolt and then, only on non-splined-spindle models, install the dust cap or the plastic ring.

5. After an hour's cycling, re-tighten the bolt; and once more after another 4 hours' use—and immediately anytime it seems to be getting loose (e.g., if you hear creaking sounds).

HOLLOWTECH NOTE:

On hollow-spindle cranksets, only the left-hand crank is removed, whereas the right-hand crank remains attached to the hollow spindle. To remove, undo the two Allen bolts on the right hand crank and slip the crank off by pulling it out away from the spindle. Then the entire unit of right-hand crank and spindle can be pulled out from the other side.

To install, push the spindle back in and clamp the left-hand crank back on with moderate hand force.

ONE-KEY CRANK ATTACHMENT NOTE:

If what looks like a dust cap around an 8 mm Allen bolt has two round recesses, it's probably the splined variety with a one-key release. On these, loosening the Allen bolt far enough actually pushes the crank off. Don't remove that thing that

Above: Fig. 10.11 Overview of hollow- spindle crankset and bottom bracket unit.

Right: Fig. 10.12. Cross-section of conventional bottom bracket. More commonly, the bearings are integrated in a cartridge unit.

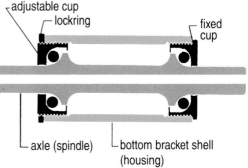

adjustable cup
lockring
fixed cup
axle (spindle)
bottom bracket shell (housing)

10

looks like a dust cap (you'd use a pin wrench to do so) because it is actually a restraint against which the crank bolt pushes to remove the crank, and you would have a hard time removing the crank if it were gone.

THE BOTTOM BRACKET

The bottom bracket is installed in the bottom bracket shell, i.e., the short piece of large-diameter tubing that runs perpendicular to the other tubes at the point where the seat tube, the down tube, and the chain stays come together. It is the most heavily loaded set of ball bearings of the bike. The cranks are attached on either side.

These days, the bottom bracket is usually a self-contained unit, or cartridge, that gets installed in one piece. Older bottom brackets may be of the type that has separate cup-and-cone bearings, which (unlike the bearings of a cassette-type bottom bracket) can be adjusted, lubricated, and overhauled. These are referred to as BSA-type bottom brackets.

MAINTENANCE OF ADJUSTABLE BOTTOM BRACKET

This is the type of older bottom bracket found on older bikes, built before the universal use of cartridge bottom brackets. These are in no way inferior and have the advantage of being adjustable. The procedure described below is for their maintenance, and should be carried out if the bearings feel either loose or tight.

If they're loose, adjusting may be enough, but if they're tight, you should also lubricate the bearings. Adjusting can be done with the cranks still installed, while the left-hand crank must be removed to lubricate or overhaul the bear-

10

Above: Fig. 10.13. Lubricating conventional bottom bracket bearing.

Right: Fig. 10.14. Replacing a typical modern cartridge bottom bracket unit.

ings. See the preceding procedure for instructions on removing and reinstalling the cranks.

TOOLS AND EQUIPMENT:

- special bottom bracket tools
- ball bearing grease and cloth (if the bearing is to be lubricated or overhauled)

ADJUSTING PROCEDURE:

1. Using the matching tool, unscrew the notched lockring on the left-hand side of the bottom bracket by about one turn.

2. Using the pin wrench of the bottom bracket tools, tighten or loosen the left-hand bearing cup about ⅛ of a turn.

3. Holding the bearing cup with the pin wrench, tighten the lockring firmly, making sure the bearing cup does not accidentally turn with it.

4. Check to make sure the adjustment is correct now and repeat if necessary.

DISASSEMBLY PROCEDURE:

1. After at least the left-hand crank has been removed (preferably also the right-hand crank, and if not, then at least remove the chain off the chainring before you start), use the matching tool to remove the lockring on the left-hand side.

2. Using the pin wrench, remove the bearing cup on the left-hand side.

3. Remove the bearing balls (usually held in a retainer) on the left-hand side.

4. Pull out the bottom bracket spindle from the right-hand side, and catch

Above: Fig. 10.15. Inserting spline tool for removal or installation of cartridge bottom bracket bearing.

Right: Fig. 10.16. Parts of a cartridge bearing assembly—but usually, you won't be able to disassemble it, and have to replace it in its entirety.

the bearing balls (also usually in a retainer) on the right-hand side. Also remove the plastic sleeve that's usually installed inside the bottom bracket shell to keep dirt from the seat tube out of the bearings.

5. Unless you really want to replace the entire unit, stop here. Otherwise, also remove the bearing cup on the right-hand side, using the matching tool. Beware that this bearing usually has left-hand screw thread (except on some French bikes), so you have to turn it clockwise to remove it.

OVERHAULING PROCEDURE:

1. Clean and inspect all components and replace any damaged, pitted, or corroded items (it's a good idea to always replace the ball bearings, available as complete sets in retainers).

    The left-hand bearing cup can be inspected while on the bike—use a light to see the condition of the bear-

ing surface—but it would have to be removed and replaced if it is damaged or badly worn (see step 5 of the disassembly procedure above).

2. Fill the bearing cups with bearing grease and make sure the screw threads of bottom bracket shell, bearing cup(s), and lockring are clean; then apply some lubricant (preferably anti-seize lubricant) to the screw-threads.

3. Insert the bearing balls with the retainer in the grease-filled bearing cups, with the continuous side of the retainer facing into the bearing cup (facing out on the assembled bike).

4. Insert the bottom bracket spindle from the left-hand side, followed by the plastic sleeve that is usually installed inside the shell to keep dirt out of the bearings.

10

Fig. 10.17. Tightening the crank bolt on a non-Hollowtech crankset.

5. Screw the left-hand bearing cup into the bottom bracket shell until the bearing is almost tight.

6. Screw the lockring over the left-hand bearing cup and hold the latter with the pin wrench while tightening the lockring with the special wrench.

7. Check the bearing adjustment for smooth running before the cranks are installed, for play after the cranks are installed, and adjust if required.

REPLACE BOTTOM BRACKET CARTRIDGE

10

Do this work if a cartridge bearing bottom bracket is loose or does not turn smoothly. On conventional units, both cranks must be removed first. However on modern hollow-spindle units, only the left-hand crank is removed.

TOOLS AND EQUIPMENT:

• special bottom bracket tool(s) for the make and model in question
• special lockring wrench

REMOVAL PROCEDURE:

1. Compare the two sides of the bottom bracket. On some, both sides have a separate lockring screwed over the top of a screw-threaded bearing adaptor. Others have only one lockring, while there's a one-piece adaptor on the other side. If there's only one lockring, note whether it's on the left-hand or right-hand side. In that case you must start assembly or disassembly from the side with the lockring.

2. Remove the lockring on the left-hand side if it's a unit with two lockrings or has the lockring on the left. If it's a single-lockring unit with the lockring on the right, remove that lockring.

3. Unscrew the second lockring (if there is a lockring on the other side as well).

4. Unscrew the body of the bearing unit: if it's a single-lockring unit, always from the side opposite the

Fig. 10.18. The chainring assembly, attached to the right-hand crank, seen here from underneath the bike.

lockring; if it's a double-lockring unit, always from the chain side.

NOTE:

If working from the right, you'll usually be dealing with left-hand thread (so you have to turn clockwise to remove, counterclockwise to install).

INSTALLATION PROCEDURE:

1. Make sure the new unit is designed for the same configuration as the old one and has the same spindle length.

2. Clean and lightly lubricate (preferably with anti-seize lubricant) all screw

threads, both in the bottom bracket shell and on the cartridge unit.

3. Screw the unit in from the left side).
   • If it's a single-lockring type, until the flange on the cartridge is hard up against the face of the bottom bracket shell.
   • If it's a double-lockring type, until the thread projects equally far on both sides.

4. Install the lockring (or both lockring if it's a double-lockring model) and tighten well, holding the body of the unit with the matching pin wrench.

5. If it's a model with two lockrings, adjust the amount of projection on the two sides to be well balanced, or to get as close as possible to the most direct (sometimes called "ideal") chain line (see Chapter 11).

10

Above: Fig. 10.19. The Allen bolts on the right-hand Hollowtech crank inserted from either side must be tightened evenly after the plastic cap (see Fig. 10.20) is screwed in to adjust the bearing.

Right: Fig. 12.20. The plastic cap serves to adjust the bearing after the crank bolts are loosened.

HOLLOWTECH NOTE:

On hollow-spindle units, the bearings are outside the bottom bracket shell. The spindle is pulled out of the bottom bracket unit from the right-hand side and remains attached to the right-hand crank. The lockrings on either side of the bottom bracket are marked with arrows to show which one is tightened clockwise, and which one counterclockwise.

The bearings are adjusted by means of the little plastic cap in the left-hand crank attachment after the crank bolts are loosened. Then tighten the crank bolts on the split crank attachment.

10

THE CHAINRINGS

Three chainrings are installed on the right-hand crank. They usually come in a standard combination with respect to the numbers of teeth. They must be designed for the particular make and model of the crankset, because the number of attachment bolts, as well as the distance relative to each other, can differ quite a bit.

Under normal circumstances, the chainrings do not wear very much and will hold up quite long. However, they may have to be replaced if they see a lot of hard use, especially in bad weather and muddy terrain—or if they get damaged.

TIGHTEN CHAINRING

In conjunction with the annual inspection (and preferably even the monthly inspection), the chainrings may have to be tightened if one or more of the installation bolts is loose. It's also one of the possible causes for unpredictable shifting of the derailleur gears.

TOOLS AND EQUIPMENT:

- Allen wrench and a slotted wrench specifically designed to fit the attachment bolts

PROCEDURE:

1. Holding each of the bolts in the back of the chainring in turn with the slotted wrench, tighten the corresponding Allen bolt from the front, gradually working around until all bolts (usually four or five) have been tightened.
   • Replace any bolts that cannot be tightened with new ones (both parts of the bolt).
   • On triple-chainring units, there is usually a second set of bolts, accessible only from the back, holding the smallest chainring—check and tighten those bolts as well.

REPLACE CHAINRING

Do this if a chainring is damaged or worn: however, sometimes you'll merely want to remove the chainrings so you can give them a more thorough cleaning, without need to actually replace them with new ones. Do this work either with the right-hand crank still installed on the bike or with the crank removed. Remove the chain from the chainring before starting this work.

Tools and equipment:

- Allen wrench and a slotted wrench specifically designed to fit the attachment bolts

Removal procedure:

1. Holding each of the bolts in the back of the chainring in turn with the slotted wrench, loosen the corresponding Allen bolt from the front, removing both parts, gradually working around until all bolts (usually either four or five) have been removed.

   There is usually a second set of bolts, accessible only from the back, holding the smallest chainring—remove those bolts as well. If not, the whole set of three chainrings stays together as a unit.

2. Remove the chainrings, either separately (in which case there will also be spacers to catch) or as a unit.

Installation procedure:

1. Compare with the original configuration how the unit is assembled (you may have to do that before installing them to the crank's chainring attachment arms).

2. Attach one bolt (with spacer) and the other part of the bolt holding the chainring(s) to the attachment, but do not tighten it fully yet.

3. Do the same with another bolt roughly opposite the first one.

4. Install the other bolts.

Left: Fig. 10.21. Inserting the chainring attachment bolts.

Right: Fig. 10.22. Tightening chainring bolts.

5. Gradually tighten all bolts fully.

NOTES:

- Replace any bolts that cannot be tightened fully, making sure they're the right length
- On bikes with special tooth patterns, the chainrings have to stay lined up the same way. Check for an alignment mark to install them correctly

STRAIGHTEN CHAINRING

If either the chainring or one or more of the teeth are bent, you may be able to correct the situation by bending it back. But replace the chainring (or the whole riveted-together set of chainrings, if that's the way they come on your bike) if a tooth breaks or is permanently de-

formed—or when the chainring is so seriously bent that the tool won't straighten it. Before you start, remove the chain from the chainring.

TOOLS AND EQUIPMENT:

- special chainring straightening tool (or an adjustable wrench)

PROCEDURE:

1. Fit the tool exactly over the tooth or the bent section of chainring as far as it will go without also grabbing beyond the location of the bend, and then use it to straighten it.

2. Check the result and repeat if necessary.

Left: Fig. 12.23. Hollowtech bottom bracket with external bearings.

Above: Fig. 12.24. Use this special tool, or a tightly adjusted Crescent wrench, to straighten any bent teeth.

11
CHAIN MAINTENANCE

The bicycle chain consists of an array of chain links, connected by means of pins. Each neighboring set of link pins is connected with side plates, and there are bushings around the pins to minimize friction.

The nominal size of a derailleur chain is ½ x ³/₃₂ inch (meaning each link is ½ inch long between pins and ³/₃₂ inch wide. However, it is no longer as standardized as it once was. With the advent of 9- and 10-speed freewheel cassettes, there is less space between them to accommodate a normal chain, so chains for these are narrower between the inner link plates (for terminology, see Fig. 11.3).

When replacing a chain, or when adding links to an existing chain, it will be very important to get one that is identical, and that may involve not only the width, but also the design of the

Left: Fig. 11.1. The chain connects the chainrings in front with the sprockets on the freewheel in the back.

Above: Fig. 11.2. Chain lubrication.

chain. The big word to keep in mind is "Hyperglide" (often abbreviated to HG)— that's the standard for Shimano's narrow specially-shaped freewheel cogs, and the chain for bikes thus equipped must be "Hyperglide compatible."

The way the ends of the chain are connected is the same way as in which all the pins connect subsequent links. To connect or disconnect the derailleur chain, one of the pins is pushed out far enough to free the inside link plate and back in again. To shorten a chain, a pin is pushed out all the way, so the last one or more links on the other side of that pin just drop out.

CHAIN LINE

That's the path the chain takes relative to the centerline through the length of the bike. Although there's no perceptible loss in efficiency, the chain is least troublesome when it runs exactly parallel. In reality, it will vary quite a bit from this "ideal" chain line when you shift gears

on a derailleur bike, making it marginally less efficient.

To keep these variations to an acceptable minimum (and more importantly, to aid gear shifting), the chain should preferably be run so that it follows the ideal chain line when the center between the two or three chainrings is lined up with the center between the biggest and smallest cog in the back.

GENERAL CHAIN MAINTENANCE

As far as chain maintenance is concerned, the main things to consider are cleaning, lubrication, and the amount of wear (which leads to apparent "stretch"). If you ride off-road in dusty or muddy terrain a lot, the chain should probably be replaced every six months or so; otherwise, once a year should be enough.

To check for wear, recommended at least once a year, use either a special chain wear tool or measure a 50-link stretch of chain to see whether it has apparently "stretched" to the point where it's 25½ inches, rather than the 25 inches a new 50-link section should measure.

The best way to clean a chain is to remove it and rinse it out in a mixture of solvent with 5–10% mineral oil, brushing and rinsing it thoroughly. Then hang it out to dry (the mineral oil that was dissolved stays behind, inhibiting rust when the solvent evaporates). In dry climates, the best lubricants are wax-based, whereas in wet weather you're

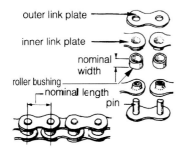

Fig. 11.3. Drawing of the parts of a typical mountain bike chain.

1 1

better off with a grease-based lubricant for the chain. The easiest way to apply the lubricant is with a spray can or a special dispenser with a brush at the end.

As a result of an accident or mal-treatment of the bike (e.g., when trans-porting or storing it), one or more links of a chain may be bent or twisted. This will seriously affect shifting on a derailleur bike—replace the links in question or the entire chain.

CHAIN REPLACEMENT

This work is required if the old chain is worn and in order to clean the existing chain. As for which chain to choose, that depends on the type and number of cogs on the back. Consult with a bike shop to make sure you get a chain suitable for the combination of cogs on your bike.

TOOLS AND EQUIPMENT:

- chain rivet tool

- cloths

REMOVAL PROCEDURE:

1. While turning the cranks by the ped-als, with the rear wheel lifted off the ground, select the gear in which the chain runs over the smallest cog in the rear and the smallest chainring in the front.

2. Turn back the handle of the chain rivet tool (counterclockwise), so the pin of the tool is retracted all the way. Then place the tool between two links, with the pin of the tool firmly up against the chain link pin.

3. Turn the handle in (clockwise) firmly, pushing the chain link pin out; but don't push the pin out all the way (it will be practically impos-sible to replace the pin if you push it out all the way)—just far enough so

11

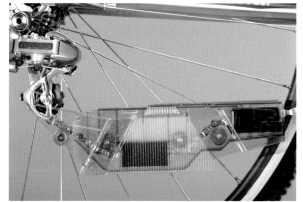

Left: Fig. 11.4. Use of special chain cleaning tool.

Above: Fig. 11.5. Close-up of the pin being pushed out with the chain tool.

no more than 1/32 inch (about 0.5 mm) of the pin stays engaged.

4. Turn the handle back (counterclock-wise) until it comes free of the chain, and remove the tool.

5. Wiggle the chain links apart at the point of the retracted chain link pin.

INSTALLATION PROCEDURE:

1. Select the gear by which the chain en-gages the smallest cog in the back and the smallest chainring in the front.

2. Working from the chain end that does not have the pin sticking out, wrap the chain around the chainring, through the front derailleur cage, around the small rear cog, and over and between the derailleur pulleys as shown in Fig. 11.6, until the two ends of the chain can be connected.

3. Place the slight inward protrusion of the pin that was pushed out over the inner link that forms the other end of the chain, and hold the two parts in place correctly aligned.

4. Turn the handle of the chain tool back far enough for the pin on the tool to clear the protruding end of the pin on the chain, and then turn it in until there is firm contact between the two pins.

5. While continuing to hold the two chain links properly aligned, turn the handle of the chain tool in, pushing the chain link pin in all the way until it protrudes equally far on both sides; then remove the tool.

6. Apply sideways force, twisting in both directions, until the two chain links around the newly replaced pin rotate freely. If it can't be done this way, put the chain tool on from the opposite side and push the chain link pin back in slightly.

• On relatively wide chains (i.e., those not intended for use with 8-or 9-speed cassettes), the connection can usually be loosened by using the chain tool in its second position, which pushes the links apart.

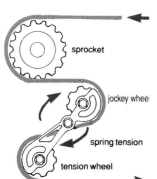

sprocket

jockey wheel

spring tension

tension wheel

Left: Fig. 11.6. Chain routing around sprockets and pulleys at rear derailleur.

Right: Fig. 11. 7. Close-up of reinserting the pin on a Hyperglide chain.

NOTE:

If the pin is accidentally pushed all the way out during disassembly, you can remove the last two links and replace them with a new two-link section of chain—taking care not to lose the pin again.

HYPERGLIDE NOTE:

On Shimano's Hyperglide chains, there is one slightly bigger link with a black finish. That's the only pin to disconnect and connect the chain (of course, to shorten the chain, you'll break it at a different link, but you'll still connect at the black pin). That pin has to be discarded when removed and replaced by a new one, which has an extension that has to be cut off after installation.

Use Shimano's special tool for working on Hyperglide chains, and keep a couple of spare black pins around.

CHAIN LENGTH

The chain should be just long enough to wrap around the biggest chainring and the biggest cog, while still leaving enough spring tension at the derailleur—and short enough not to hang loose while it runs over the smallest cog and the smallest chainring. (If that can't be achieved, you need a rear derailleur on which the pulleys are farther apart, known as a wide-range or long-cage derailleur.)

Major corrections of the chain length are made by removing or adding a section of chain consisting of an even number of links. Follow essentially the same procedure described above for chain removal and installation.

11

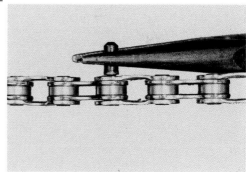

Left: Fig. 11.8. The pin pushed out far enough to "break" the chain.

Above: Fig. 11.9. Snapping off the HG pin extension.

12 Pedal Maintenance

Pedals come in two basic types: conventional and clipless. Conventional pedals can be used with regular footwear, while clipless pedals require special shoes equipped with matching clips. (Yes, "clipless" is a bit of a misnomer for something that actually requires a special clip attached to the shoe sole.)

Pedal Types

They also come with one of two bearing types: cartridge or cup-and-cone bearings. You can tell them apart as follows: If there's a removable dust cap on the outside end of the pedal, it's probably a conventional (adjustable) type; if not, it's definitely a cartridge-bearing type.

Clipless pedals always have cartridge bearings, while conventional pedals may be of either type.

Left: Fig. 12.1. Typical clipless pedal with cartridge bearings.

Above: Fig. 12.2. Conventional pedal with cup-and-cone bearing.

The pedals are screwed into the threaded holes at the end of the cranks. The left-hand pedal has left-hand screw thread (and is usually marked with an "L"), while the right-hand pedal has regular right-hand screw thread. If you're having difficulty tightening or loosening a pedal, first check whether you're turning them the right way or not—left-hand thread means tighten counterclockwise and loosen clockwise. And remember that the right-hand crank is the one on the chain side.

Pedal adjustment or overhauling will be called for if the pedal either feels loose or does not turn freely. If it wobbles, there's a more serious problem—the spindle is bent. In that case, replace either the pedal spindle (if available) or the whole pedal.

The release force of clipless pedals can be adjusted to suit your needs. If you use conventional pedals, you may want to use them in conjunction with "old-fashioned" toe-clips. Check and tighten their attachment screws to the front of the pedal occasionally to stop them from coming loose.

When a bike comes from the store, it may be equipped with clipless pedals that are covered with a plastic device incorporating reflectors and allowing one side of the pedal to be used with normal street shoes. My advice is to remove those plastic devices and either use the clipless pedals with matching shoes or to install regular pedals, both sides of which are suitable for use with street shoes. To remove it, twist it sideways and up from the pedal to dislodge it from the pedal's retention mechanism.

12

Above: Fig. 12.3. Removal or installation of pedal using a pedal wrench.

Right: Fig. 12.4. The same procedure using an Allen wrench from the back of the crank.

The other items you'll often find on a conventional pedal are little reflectors. Also check and tighten their attachments from time to time, and replace them if missing or broken.

With all pedal work, you should work on only one at a time. That's because some identical-looking parts of the two pedals are actually not identical and you would do serious damage if you mixed them up.

REPLACE PEDALS

This work can be called for if the pedal is damaged—or when the bike has to be stored in a small box, e.g., to be transported. Note that the pedal wrench used for this work may either be the metric size 15 mm or the non-metric size $9/16$ inch.

TOOLS AND EQUIPMENT:

- pedal wrench (or, if not too tight, a (preferably long) 6 mm Allen wrench)
- lubricant
- cloth

REMOVAL PROCEDURE:

1. Place the pedal wrench on the flat surfaces of the stub between the pedal and the crank. (If the pedal is not on too tight, it can usually be done with the Allen wrench, reaching the hexagonal recess that's present in the end of most modern pedals from the back of the crank.)

2. Hold the crank arm firmly and:
    • for the right-hand pedal, turn counterclockwise to loosen

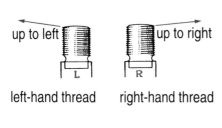

left-hand thread   right-hand thread

Above: Fig. 12.5. How to tell which pedal goes on the left and which one goes on the right.

Right: Fig. 12.6. Whatever the type of pedal you use, lubricate the pedal thread before installing it (and don't forget to clean the screw-thread first).

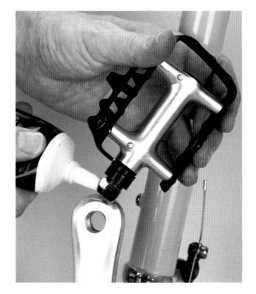

1 2

• for the left-hand pedal, turn clockwise

3. Unscrew the pedal all the way.

INSTALLATION PROCEDURE:

1 Clean the thread surfaces in the cranks and on the pedals, and lubricate them lightly.

2. Carefully align the thread of the pedal stub with the thread in the crank and start screwing it in by hand (counterclockwise for the left-hand pedal).

3. Screw in the pedal fully with the pedal wrench (or from the back of the crank, using the Allen wrench). There's no need to tighten them excessively.

ADJUST RELEASE FORCE OF CLIPLESS PEDAL

If it is too hard to get your foot out of a clipless pedal, or if it does not hold the shoe firmly enough, you can adjust the spring tension.

TOOLS AND EQUIPMENT:

• Allen wrench to fit the adjustment bolt(s)

PROCEDURE

1. Locate the tension adjustment bolt or bolts on the pedal in question.

2. Tighten or loosen the bolt(s) as required.

3. Check operation and fine-tune adjustment if necessary.

12

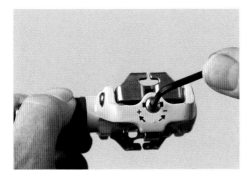

Above: Fig. 12.7. Unscrewing the cartridge assembly from the housing of a cartridge-bearing pedal.

Right: Fig. 12.8. A conventional pedal with cup-and-cone bearings disassembled.

ADJUST CONVENTIONAL PEDAL BEARINGS

This work can usually be done with the pedal still attached to the bike. However, if the pedal has a cage that wraps around, it may be necessary to remove the cage to gain access to the outboard bearing.

TOOLS AND EQUIPMENT:

- tool to remove dust cap
- open-ended wrench and/or socket wrench
- small screwdriver

Above: Fig. 12.9. Cage removed from conventional pedal. That only works on high-end pedals, because cheap pedals come in one piece.

Right: Fig. 12.10. The adjustable end of a conventional-bearing pedal, shown here after removing the dustcap and the locknut.

PROCEDURE:

1. Holding the pedal at the crank, loosen the dust cap (it's usually threaded but may be snapped on, in which case you'll have to pry it off).

2. Unscrew the locknut by about one turn.

3. Using whatever tool fits the cone (the small screwdriver if the top of the cone is slotted), turn the cone in or out by about ¼ turn to tighten or loosen the bearing respectively.

4. Holding the cone with the screwdriver, tighten the locknut.

5. Check the adjustment of the bearing and fine-tune the adjustment if necessary, making sure the locknut is firmed up properly.

6. Reinstall the dust cap.

OVERHAUL CONVENTIONAL PEDAL

Although this work can be done with the pedal still on the bike, it's recommended to remove it first—and reinstall it afterwards. As mentioned in the adjusting procedure, you may have to remove the cage to lubricate the outboard bearing.

Because some pedal parts are not interchangeable between left and right, you should keep all the parts separate or work on only one pedal at a time.

TOOLS AND EQUIPMENT:

- tool to remove dust cap
- open-ended wrench and/or socket wrench
- small screwdriver
- cloth
- bearing grease

DISASSEMBLY PROCEDURE:

1. Holding the pedal at the crank, loosen the dust cap (it's usually threaded, but may be snapped on, in which case you'll be able to pry it off).

2. Unscrew the locknut and remove it; then also remove the keyed washer.

3. Using whatever tool fits the cone (the small screwdriver if the top of the cone is slotted), unscrew and remove the cone.

4. Pull the pedal body and the pedal spindle apart, catching all the bearing balls.

OVERHAULING AND REASSEMBLY PROCEDURE:

1. Clean and inspect all parts, replacing any that are pitted, corroded, or otherwise damaged. It's always a good idea to replace the bearing balls, which on pedals are not held in a retainer.

2. Fill both bearing cups with bearing grease, and push the bearing balls in.

3. Slide the pedal body back over the spindle, with the larger bearing cup toward the crank. Be careful not to push the ball bearings out.

1 2

Fig. 12.11. Bearing cartridge removed from the housing of a clipless cartridge-bearing pedal.

4. Install the cone until the bearing feels just barely loose.

5. Install the keyed washer with the tab matching the groove (replace it if it is worn so much that it can slip out of the groove).

6. Install the locknut and tighten it against the cone.

7. Check the bearing adjustment and fine-tune it if necessary.

8. Install the dust cap.

MAINTENANCE OF CARTRIDGE-BEARING PEDAL

You can do this work either with the pedal still installed on the bike or removed. Because some pedal parts are not interchangeable between left and right, you should keep all the parts separate or work on only one pedal at a time.

TOOLS AND EQUIPMENT:

- wrench to fit the flat hexagonal stub that screws into the pedal body
- cloth
- lubricant

DISASSEMBLY PROCEDURE

1. Holding the hexagonal stub that's screwed into the back of the pedal body with the wrench, unscrew the pedal body off by hand. (It may have either right-or left-hand screw thread.)

2. Pull off the pedal body. You have now separated the pedal spindle with one (inner) bearing from the pedal body with the other (outer) bearing.

3. Check to see whether there is access to the pedal body that allows you to remove the outer bearing—and do so if you can (otherwise, a special tool will be needed, and you should leave this job to a bike mechanic).

12

Fig. 12.12. Unscrewing the cartridge assembly from the housing of a cartridge-bearing pedal.

OVERHAULING AND ASSEMBLY PROCEDURE:

1. Check the condition of any parts you can see. If the spindle is bent, replace the entire cartridge (if available—if not, you'll have to replace the pedals).

2. If you can remove the bearings, do so. If not, try to lift the bearing seals to gain access to them.

3. Lubricate the bearings and reinstall the parts on the spindle, or spindle.

4. Reinstall any parts you removed and reinsert the cartridge into the pedal body.

5. Screw the cartridge in all the way.

ADJUSTING SHOE PLATES

Clipless pedals must be used with special matching shoes, and the Shimano SPD system for pedals and shoes is the universal standard for mountain bikes. Follow this procedure to adjust them properly.

TOOLS AND EQUIPMENT:

- 5 mm Allen wrench

ADJUSTING PROCEDURE:

1. Wearing the shoe, establish the center of the ball of the foot and mark it with a line with a felt-tip pen on the side of the sole.

2. Take off the shoe and loosen the Allen bolts that hold the cleat to the shoe by about one turn—just enough to force the cleat's position by hand, but not loose.

3. Place the shoe on the pedal with the cleat engaged in the clip of the pedal, and check the location of the line relative to the center of the pedal. Shift the shoe plate relative to the shoe until it is above the center of the pedal, keeping the shoe parallel to the crank.

4. Tighten the bolts and test ride the bike. If you detect sideways angular

1 2

Fig. 12.13. Removable platform to convert a clipless pedal for use with regular footwear.

movement in the knee, you have to fine-tune the adjustment to shift the heel of the shoe in or out a little. Repeat until comfortable.

CONVERTIBLE PEDALS

Some pedals have a clipless mechanism, combined with a platform that is held on around it for use with normal shoes.

To get the benefit of the clipless mechanism, you can remove the outer part. First release the spring tension of the clipless mechanism, then use a small screwdriver to pry the platform out of the clamp of the clipless mechanism.

TOECLIPS

Conventional pedals lend themselves to the installation of toeclips, which gives the same advantage as clipless pedals without the need for special shoes.

Use a screwdriver and a small wrench to install the clips. Then thread the strap through with the buckle on the outside of the pedal, and twisting it as shown in Fig. 12.14.

You may be able to install a pedal reflector on both ends of the pedal (using its screws to hold down the toeclip in the front.

Fig. 12.14. Routing of toestrap on conventional pedal used with toeclips.

13 STEERING SYSTEM MAINTENANCE

The steering system comprises the handlebars, the headset bearings, the stem, and the front fork. Since most modern mountain bikes use suspension forks, the latter item will be covered in a separate chapter, while this chapter deals with the handlebars and the headset.

Mountain bikes almost invariably have flat handlebars, as opposed to the "drop" handlebars that are used on road bikes.

The handlebars are connected to the fork via a stem that is clamped to the front fork's steerer tube and around the center portion of the handlebars. On older mountain bikes, the stem fits inside the fork's steerer tube and a different type of headset is used—referred to as a threaded headset, as opposed to the threadless type used on most newer machines.

After the shifters and brake levers are installed on the handlebars, the flat bars

Right: Fig. 13.1. The bare essentials of a mountain bike steering system, shown here on a bike without suspension.

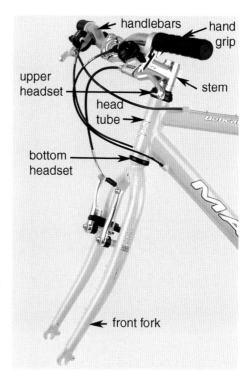

get equipped with handgrips pushed over the ends.

ADJUST HANDLEBAR HEIGHT

Unfortunately, this simplest of all handlebar adaptations only works on (old) bikes with a conventional threaded headset. On today's bikes with a threadless headset, the only way to raise or lower the handlebars is by means of installing a different stem).

Fig. 13.2. Clamping in the front end of the bike when working on the steering system.

TOOLS AND EQUIPMENT:

- Allen wrench (or, for older low-end bikes, regular wrench)
- mallet (or a hammer and a protective block of wood)

PROCEDURE:

1. Clamp the front wheel between your legs from the front and loosen the binder bolt on top of the stem by about 5 turns.

2. Tap on the bolt with a mallet (or a hammer, protecting the bolt with a block of wood) to loosen the wedge inside the stem—the bolt will drop down, loosening the stem.

3. Raise or lower the handlebars as desired and hold them there firmly.

4. Check to make sure the marking that shows the maximum extension of the stem does not show above the headset (and if it does, lower the stem until it doesn't, because raising it too high might cause it to break or come loose).

5. Holding the handlebars at the desired height and straight (still clamping the front wheel between your legs), tighten the bolt on top of the stem firmly.

13

NOTES:

A. At least 2½ inches (6.5 cm) of the stem must remain clamped in. Usually, the stem is marked for this insertion depth, but even if it's not, that's the minimum for safety.

B. On modern mountain bikes, with a threadless headset, the handlebar height can only be changed by installing a different stem—available with different amounts of rise, as will be covered below under *Replace Stem*.

ADJUST HANDLEBAR ANGLE

This adjustment allows you to find a more comfortable rotation of the handlebars, if needed.

TOOLS AND EQUIPMENT:

• Allen wrench

PROCEDURE:

1. Undo the clamp bolt(s) that hold the stem clamp around the handlebars by about one turn.

2. Turn the handlebars into the desired orientation, making sure they remain centered on the stem.

3. Holding the bars in the desired orientation and location, tighten the stem clamp bolt(s).

REPLACE HANDLEBARS

Do this work if the handlebars are damaged in a fall or simply because you want to try a different type. Before pro-

13

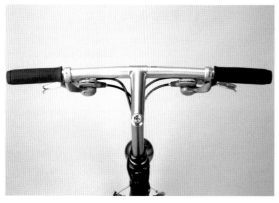

Above: Fig. 13.3. Older style steering system with conventional headset.

Right: Fig. 13.4. Loosening the stem on a bike with a threaded headset to adjust the handlebar height.

ceeding, make sure the new handlebars actually fit the stem that's installed on the bike (or replace the stem as well—see *Replace Stem* below.

TOOLS AND EQUIPMENT:

• Allen wrench and whatever tools are needed to remove items installed on the handlebars.

PROCEDURE:

1. Remove anything installed on the handlebars (such as brake levers, gear shifters, handgrips, etc.).

2. Unscrew the bolt(s) that hold the clamp on the stem around the center section of the handlebars.

3. Pull the handlebars out, wiggling and rotating them until they come out. (You may have to pry open the clamp with the aid of a large screwdriver or a coin to get enough clearance.)

4. Tighten the clamp bolt(s) when the handlebars are in the right location and orientation.

5. Reinstall all items that were removed in step 1.

REPLACE STEM

This operation may be needed if the stem that's on the bike brings the handlebars too far forward or not far enough, or in combination with a threadless headset, too low or too high. If it's too long, you want one with less "reach"; if it's too low, one with more "rise." Make sure you get a replacement stem of the same general type (i.e., for the same type and size of steerer tube and the same diameter handlebars).

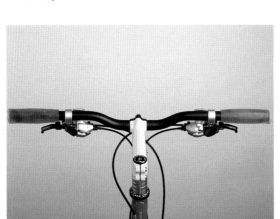

Left: Fig. 13.5. Steering system with threadless headset.

Above: Fig. 13.6. Loosening or tightening stem clamp bolt on threadless headset.

You'll also have to remove the handlebars from the stem and reinstall them when you've finished, following the preceding procedure *Replace Handlebars*.

Tools and equipment:

- Allen wrenches
- for threaded headset: cloth and lubricant and a mallet (or a hammer and a protective block of wood)

Procedure:

1. Establish whether this is a bike with a threaded or threadless headset (compare the illustrations Figs. 13.3 and 13.5).
   • On a threaded headset, undo the bolt on top of the stem (see Fig. 13.4) by about 5 turns and then tap on the bolt with a mallet (or a hammer and a protective block of wood) to loosen the stem.
   • On a threadless headset, first undo the Allen bolt on the top of the stem, which is only an adjusting bolt (see Fig. 13.6), then remove this bolt and the underlying plastic cap, and finally loosen the clamp bolts that clamp the stem around the fork's steerer tube extension that sticks out above the upper headset bearing.

2. Remove the old stem.

3. Open the bolts on the new stem (if it's for a threaded headset: far enough so the wedge is loose enough to line up perfectly with the stem without touching it).
   • On a threaded headset, place the new stem in place (first put some lubricant on the screw-threaded portion of the bolt and the wedge or cone), and orient it properly.
   • On a threadless headset, put the stem in place, after installing any spacers required; but don't tighten the bolts that clamp it around the fork's smooth steerer tube extension yet. Install the cap and the bolt on top, and use the bolt to adjust the headset, and only then tighten those clamp bolts.

4. While firmly holding the handlebars in place, tighten the bolt(s).

5. After you've installed the handlebars, make any final adjustments necessary.

13

Fig. 13.7. Loosening stem clamp to adjust handlebar rotation or remove handlebars.

REPLACE HANDGRIPS

Do this if the old grips are not comfortable—or if you have to replace the brake lever, the gear shifter, the handlebars, or the stem.

TOOLS AND EQUIPMENT:

- screwdriver
- sometimes hot water, dishwashing liquid, hair spray, and/or a knife

PROCEDURE:

1. Remove the old handgrips by pulling and twisting—if they do not come off easily, place the screwdriver under the old grip and let some dishwashing liquid enter between the grip and the handlebars. If all else fails, cut the grip lengthwise and "peel" it off.

2. Push the new handgrips over the ends of the handlebars. If they don't go on easily, soak them in warm water first. To make them adhere better, you can spray some hair spray inside the grips just before installing them.

INSTALL BAR-ENDS

Bar-ends are forward pointing extensions that can be installed at the ends of mountain bike handlebars to offer the rider an additional, for some more comfortable, riding position. They're clamped around the ends of the handlebars. Since these things may form a potential hazard in a fall if they stick straight out, look for a model that curves in and has flexible protection at the ends.

13

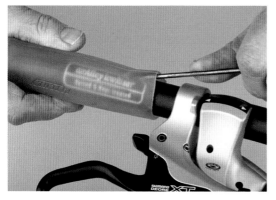

Above: Fig. 13.8. Replacing handgrip.

Right: Fig. 13.9. Installing or replacing bar-ends.

Tools and equipment:

- Allen wrench

Procedure:

1. Remove the existing handgrips, and replace them with open-ended grips, pushed about ¾ inch (2 cm) further to the center of the bars. (Alternately, you can cut the ends off the existing ones and slide them in that far).

2. Place the bar ends over the uncovered ends of the handlebars, with the clamping bolts underneath—the extensions pointing forward and slightly up (by about 15–30 degrees).

3. Tighten the clamp bolts very firmly, while making sure both point up at the same angle.

4. Ride the bike and do any fine-tuning that may be necessary.

Headset Maintenance

The headset is the center of the bike's steering system. The two types (threaded and threadless) are illustrated in detail in Figs. 13.10 and 13.16. Each consists of upper and lower sets of ball bearings, mounted in the top and the bottom of the frame's head tube respectively. The type referred to as "integrated headset" is merely a variant of the threadless type.

Unlike other bearings on the bike, these get most of their work without rotating much—from road shocks parallel to their axis, resulting in more wear. Consequently, the bearings may need replacing once a year.

Most modern mountain bikes threadless headset, often referred to by

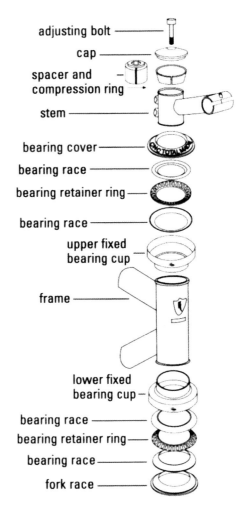

Fig. 13.10. Exploded view of threadless headset and stem assembly.

13

the trade name AHeadset. It is adjusted from the top of the handlebar stem.

Older bikes have a threaded headset, which is not really inferior – just out of fashion. This type has a screw-threaded adjustable bearing race that is screwed onto the fork's steerer tube.

There is also something called an integrated headset, which is similar to the threadless bearing but consists of fewer parts, sitting directly in the frame's head tube. Comparing the illustrations will help you define which type is installed on the bike you're working on.

Maintenance work on the headset includes adjusting, overhauling, and replacing the bearings. These operations are different for the two major types of headsets. Some of this work also has to be carried out when you have to replace e.g., the front fork.

Fig. 13.11. Stem cap and top bolt removed on bike with threadless headset.

OVERHAUL OR REPLACE THREADLESS HEADSET

The threadless headset requires a special fork, which does not have screw thread on the steerer tube (hence the name). The bolt on top of the stem does not hold the parts together, but is merely there for adjustment of the bearing. Before you start, unhook the front brake cable and remove the front wheel.

TOOLS AND EQUIPMENT:

- Allen wrenches
- cloth
- bearing grease

DISASSEMBLY PROCEDURE:

1. Undo the Allen bolt on top of the stem and remove it, together with the underlying cap.

2. Holding the fork and the bottom of the head tube together, loosen the bolts that clamp the stem around the top portion of the fork's steerer tube; then remove the stem.

3. Pull the fork out of the head tube, catching the bearing balls.

OVERHAULING PROCEDURE:

1. Clean and inspect all parts, and replace any parts that are damaged, corroded, pitted, or grooved. If you have to replace individual parts or

13

the entire headset, it's best to take the fork with you to the shop to make sure you get parts of the correct size to match the fork's steerer tube diameter.

2. If you have to replace the entire headset, it will be best to have a bike shop install the fixed components (the fixed upper and lower bearing races and the fork race), because that job is best done with special tools that any bike shop should have but for which you don't have a use often enough to justify the investment.

INSTALLATION PROCEDURE:

1. Fill the upper and lower fixed bearing races with bearing grease.

2. Holding the frame upside down, put the retainer ring with the bearing balls in the lower fixed race.

3. Holding the fork upside down as well, insert the fork's steerer tube through the frame's head tube until the bearing balls of the lower headset bearing are securely held between the fork race and the lower fixed race.

4. Turn the bike the right way round, carefully holding the fork and the lower part of the head tube together.

Above: Fig. 13.12. Tightening or loosening the stem clamp bolts on a bike with a threadless headset..

Right: Fig 13.13. Stem removed on a bike with a threadless headset. Note the spacers installed to achieve a high handlebar position on this bike.

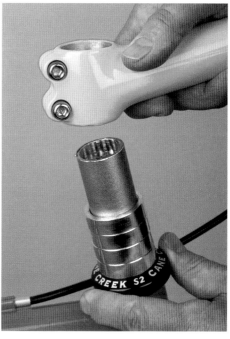

13

5. Still holding things together with one hand, first put the retainer ring with the bearing balls into the upper fixed bearing race and then slide the adjustable bearing race onto the fork's steerer tube.

6. Install the slotted, tapered ring (or two tapered segments) in the gap and place the washer on top. Install any other spacers that may be used to raise the handlebars, then slide the stem on and provisionally screw the stem clamp bolts just enough to hold things together but free to slide.

7. Install the cap on top of the stem and attach it loosely with the Allen bolt on top, screwing the latter into what the manufacturer refers to as a "star-fangled" nut inside the fork's steerer tube.

8. Adjust the bearing with the Allen bolt on top of the stem (clockwise to tighten, counterclockwise to loosen the bearing), then tighten the stem clamp bolts with the handlebars in the correct orientation.

NOTE:

- If the "star-fangled" nut is pushed too far into the steerer tube, or if it goes under an angle, you can push it out from the bottom (holding the

13

Above: Fig. 13.14. View inside the stem of a threadless headset, showing the "star-fangled washer," which is really a nut in which the top bolt engages.

Right: Fig. 13.15. The bottom end of the fork's steerer tube exposed, showing the seating for the bottom headset race (which, in this photo is still stuck in the headset cup at the bottom of the head tube).

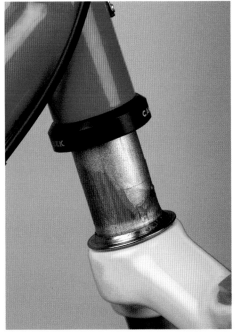

fork upside-down) with a large screwdriver and a hammer or a mallet. Then have a bike shop push it (or a replacement) in again from the top, using a special tool.

Integrated Headset Note:

• Integrated headsets work just like the threadless headset, except that the bearing races are permanently integrated with the head tube and the parts just slide into place. Adjustment, removal, overhaul, and

installation follow the same procedure, as adapted for the fewer parts that are actually there.

Adjust Threaded Headset

If the bearings are too tight or too loose, first try to adjust them. If that does not solve the problem, you'll have to proceed to the instructions for overhauling, or even replacing, the headset.

Tools and equipment:

• headset wrenches (make sure they're the size to match the make and model in question)
• sometimes a large adjustable wrench can be used as a substitute for a specific size headset wrench)
• sometimes a tiny Allen wrench, if there's a grub screw to hold down the bearing locknut

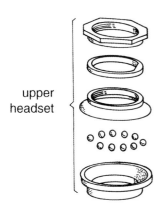

upper headset

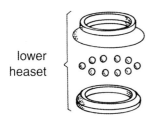

lower heaset

Above: Fig. 13.16. Exploded view of threaded headset assembly.

Right: Fig. 13.17. Adjusting threaded headset. When overhauling a headset, first remove the stem from the bike.

13

1. Loosen the locknut on top of the upper headset bearing about one turn
   (unless there is a toothed ring underneath, on some older headsets—in
   that case far enough to free those
   teeth). If the locknut is held with a
   grub screw, loosen that little screw
   before trying to undo the locknut.

2. Lift the keyed washer that lies under
   the locknut to allow the adjustable
   bearing race to be rotated.

3. Turn the adjustable bearing face in
   ⅛-turn increments (clockwise to
   tighten, counterclockwise to loosen)

Fig. 13.18. Bearing ball retainer on a
threaded headset.

until it feels just barely loose (that
slack will get taken up when the
locknut is screwed down).

4. Tighten the locknut fully, while
   holding the adjustable race with the
   other wrench.

5. Check to make sure the bearing is
   properly adjusted now, or fine-tune
   the adjustment if necessary, then
   tighten the locknut firmly.

ADJUST THREADLESS HEADSET

The threadless headset tends to stay
properly adjusted longer, but there may
still be a need for adjustment from time
to time.

TOOLS AND EQUIPMENT:

• Allen wrenches

PROCEDURE:

1. Loosen the clamp bolts that hold the
   stem around the fork's steerer tube
   by about one turn each.

2. Tighten or loosen the Allen bolt on
   top of the stem—this is not a binder
   bolt taking force but solely serves as
   an adjustment bolt (and the plastic or
   aluminum cap underneath would
   break if too much force were applied
   to it by that bolt). Tighten by turning

the bolt clockwise, loosen by turning it counterclockwise.

3. When the adjustment feels right, tighten the stem clamp bolts, making sure the handlebars are straight.

OVERHAUL OR REPLACE THREADED HEADSET

Do this work when the steering has become rough and the problem cannot be solved by simply adjusting the headset bearings in accordance with the preceding instructions.

Before starting, remove the handlebar stem from the bike. Also remove the front wheel and unhook the front brake cable.

TOOLS AND EQUIPMENT:

* headset wrenches or substitute wrenches
* sometimes a tiny Allen wrench if there's a grub screw to hold down the bearing locknut
* cloth
* bearing grease

DISASSEMBLY PROCEDURE:

1. Loosen and remove the locknut on top of the upper headset (if appropriate, after unscrewing a grub screw that may be present on some models).

2. Lift and remove the keyed washer from the fork's screw-threaded steerer tube (note that the steerer tube has a matching groove or flat spot cut into the screw thread)—that's to stop the washer from rotating.

3. Unscrew the adjustable bearing race (if necessary, after loosening a grub screw) while holding the fork and the frame together at the fork crown.

4. Remove the bearing balls from the upper fixed bearing race (usually held in a retainer).

Fig. 13.19. Keyed lock washer on a threaded headset.

13

5. Pull the fork out of the frame, catching the bearing balls (usually in a retainer) from the lower bearing race.

OVERHAULING PROCEDURE:

1. Clean and inspect all parts, replacing any parts that are damaged, corroded, pitted, or grooved. A particular problem to watch for is "brinelling" of a bearing surface, i.e., pitting caused by repeated impact at the same point (most prevalent at the lower headset bearing).
   • When replacing parts (or, for that matter, when replacing an entire headset) be aware that they come in different sizes—take the fork with you to the shop to get one that's guaranteed to fit.

Fig. 13.20. If the bearings are accessible, as in this photo, they should be cleaned and lubricated, whereas cartridge bearings may have to be replaced altogether.

2. If the entire headset has to be replaced, it will be best to have a bike shop remove and install the fixed components (the upper and lower cups on the head tube and the fork race on the fork crown), because those jobs are best done with special tools.

INSTALLATION PROCEDURE:

1. Fill the upper and lower fixed bearing races with bearing grease.

2. Holding the frame upside down, put the bearing balls (usually in a retainer) in the lower fixed race.

3. Holding the fork upside down as well, push the fork's steerer tube through until the bearing balls of the lower headset bearing are securely held between the fork race and the lower fixed race.

4. Turn the bike the right way round, carefully holding the fork crown and the lower part of the head tube together.

5. Still holding the parts together with one hand, put the bearing balls (also usually in a retainer) into the upper fixed bearing race, then screw the adjustable bearing race onto the fork's steerer tube until the bearing is just slightly loose.

6. Install the keyed washer on the adjustable bearing race, matching the

13

prong or the flat part of the washer up with the groove or flat area on the threaded portion of the steerer tube. Also install any other items that may have to go between the lock washer and the locknut (e.g., spacer or cantilever brake stop).

7. Holding the adjustable bearing cup with one tool, install and tighten the locknut fully.

8. Check whether the headset is now adjusted properly (i.e., free to rotate without resistance on the one hand or looseness on the other, and fine-tune the adjustment if necessary.

CARTRIDGE BEARING NOTE:

Some conventional-looking headsets on high-end bikes are equipped with cartridge bearings. They can't be adjustable, and you'll have to get them replaced at a bike shop if they do give you trouble (but don't worry, they can handle many years of hard use).

FORK INSPECTION

These instructions are for bikes with a conventional, non-suspension fork. With the now almost universal use of front suspension, the bending of forks is less common. If your suspension fork is bent, the tubes don't slide in-and-out properly anymore.

What matters here is the alignment of the two fork blades relative to each other

and relative to the steerer tube. On a regular fork, you can usually check the alignment by means of a visual inspection.

TOOLS AND EQUIPMENT:

- calipers
- flat, level surface

PROCEDURE:

1. Place the fork flat on the level surface, supporting it at the fork crown and the upper straight section of the fork blades.

2. Compare the distance between the level surface and the fork ends. If there's a difference, they're misaligned.

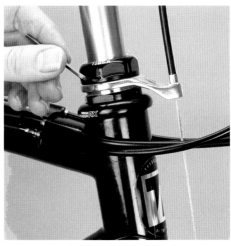

Fig. 13.21. This threaded headset has a set screw to prevent accidental loosening. Undo it before working on the headset, and tighten it again afterward.

13

3. Visually establish whether the line that goes through the center of the steerer tube also goes through the center of the upper straight portion of the fork blades. If it doesn't, you have misalignment between the fork blades and the steerer tube.

4. Also in this case, once you have established that there is misalignment, go to a bike shop and get advice on what to do.

FRONT FORK INSTALLATION

To replace the fork, first make sure that the headset fits both the new fork's steerer tube and the frame's head tube.

Not only is there the difference between threaded and threadless steerer tubes, depending on the type of headset used, there are also steerer tubes and headsets in different diameters.

Also the length of the steerer tube must add up to the height of the frame's head tube plus the "stacking height" of the headset (and the stem height plus any spacers in the case of a threadless headset).

Additionally, there's the distinction between regular forks and suspension forks. If you are trying to install a suspension fork in a frame not specifically designed for one, explain that at the bike shop before buying the fork, because for safe handling, you should avoid altering the bike's steering geometry too much.

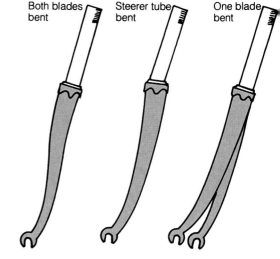

Both blades bent   Steerer tube bent   One blade bent

Above: Fig. 13.22. An irreparable kind of fork damage: bent brake mounting pivot bosses.

Right: Fig. 13.23. Three forms of possible fork damage to check for.

13

14
SEAT AND SEATPOST

T he seat, or saddle, is usually made of a firm but flexible plastic base, held on a metal frame, with a real or simulated leather cover over a thin layer of soft padding. It is attached to the frame by means of a tubular seatpost.

Seats for fast riding and quick bike handling are narrow and firm, while seats intended for an upright riding position tend to be wide and soft (or rather: not quite so rock hard). Some seats are made of self-supporting thick and firm leather, directly connected to the metal frame.

The seat is held on the bike by means of a tubular seatpost, which is clamped in at the seat lug, at the top of the frame's seat tube. Different inside diameters of seat tubes call for seatposts with (slightly) different outside diameters. The seat lug and the top of the seat tube are split in the back and tightened around the seatpost with a clamp, which is either bolted together or clamped with a quick-release device.

ADJUST SEAT HEIGHT

Once you've determined how high you want the seat to be, this is how you get it there.

Fig. 14.1. Seat and seatpost as installed on a hardtail bike

TOOLS AND EQUIPMENT:

- Depending on the type of clamp, either none (if quick-release) or an Allen wrench (if no quick-release)

PROCEDURE:

1. Depending on the type of seat clamp:
   • On a bike with a regular bolted clamp, undo the bolt (referred to as binder bolt) by 2–3 turns.
   • On a bike with quick-release clamp, twist the quick-release lever into the "open" position.

2. Try to move the seatpost up or down in a twisting movement, using the seat for leverage and holding the bike's frame. If it doesn't budge, squirt some penetrating oil in at the point where the seat lug is slotted, so it enters between the seatpost and the seat tube. Wait 2–3 minutes and try again.

3. Move it to the exact location where you want it to be, but make sure the marker that shows the minimum insertion depth is not exposed (if it is, it'll be dangerous to ride that way, and you'll need either a longer seatpost or a bigger frame).

4. Holding the seat at the right height and straight ahead, tighten the binder bolt or the quick-release. (If the quick-release can't be tightened properly, flip it to "open" again, ad-

14

Left: Fig. 14.2. Adjusting the seat height on a seatpost clamped in without quick-release on a full-suspension bike.

Above: Fig. 14.3. To adjust the seat height on a bike with quick-release, loosen the quick-release and move the seatpost up or down, rotating it from the seat if necessary.

just the thumb nut on the other side, and try again.)

5. Check to make sure the position is correct, and fine-tune the various adjustments if necessary. You may find that you now need to adjust the angle and forward position in accordance with the instructions below as well.

NOTE:

• At least 2½ inches (6.5 cm) of the seatpost must be clamped in. Usually the seatpost is marked to show this minimum safe insertion depth.

clamp); and on low-end bikes, there's one nut on both sides of the wires (or the flat rails often used on such seats).

2. Loosen the bolt(s) about 3 turns.

3. Move the seat forward or backward on the wires (while making sure the clamp does not run off those wires) and hold it at the desired location under the desired angle.

4. Holding the seat steadily in place, tighten the bolts—gradually tightening both of them in turn if there are two.

ADJUST SEAT ANGLE AND POSITION

These features are adjusted by means of one or more bolts, usually accessible from underneath the seat, that hold the seat wires to the seatpost.

TOOLS AND EQUIPMENT:

• Allen wrench (or sometimes a regular wrench for an older bike)

PROCEDURE:

1. Look under the seat and identify the bolts in question; usually they're easily accessible from below, but they can be tricky to get at on old seats (between the seat cover and the

14

Fig. 14.4. Seat and seatpost removed from the bike's seat tube.

5. Check to make sure the position is correct, and fine-tune the various adjustments if necessary (it may also have affected the height adjustment).

REPLACE SEAT

To do this work, e.g., because you want to try a more comfortable model, you can either leave the seatpost clamped in at the bike or you can work on it while it's off the bike.

TOOLS AND EQUIPMENT:

• Allen wrench (or sometimes a regular wrench on an older bike)

PROCEDURE:

1. Look under the seat and identify the bolts in question; usually they're easily accessible from below, but they can be tricky to get at on old seats.

2. Loosen the bolt or bolts (usually there are two) far enough to twist the seat off the clip.

3. Install the new seat on the clamp and hold it loosely with the bolts or nuts.

4. Move the seat forward or backward on the wires (while making sure the clamp does not run off those wires) and hold it at the desired location under the desired angle.

5. Holding the seat steadily in place, tighten the bolts—gradually tightening both of them in turn if there are two.

6. Check to make sure the position is correct, and fine-tune the various adjustments if necessary.

14

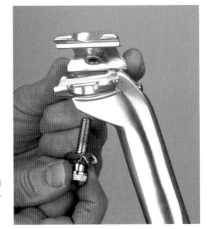

Left: Fig. 14.5. Seatpost clip disassembled.

Right: Fig. 14.6. Tightening or loosening the connection between the seat and the seatpost (this being a slightly different model seatpost).

REPLACE SEATPOST

To remove the seatpost, first leave the seat on the seatpost and remove the two together as a single unit, then take the seatpost off the seat.

TOOLS AND EQUIPMENT:

- Depending on the type of clamp, either none (if quick-release), an Allen wrench, or a regular wrench (older or low-end bike)
- cloth
- grease
- sometimes penetrating oil

PROCEDURE:

1. Depending on the type of clamp:
   • On a bike with a regular bolted clamp, undo the binder bolt 2–3 turns.

• On a bike with a quick-release clamp, twist the quick-release lever into the "open" position.

2. Try to move the seatpost up in a twisting movement, using the seat for leverage. If it doesn't budge, squirt some penetrating oil in at the point where the seat lug is slotted, so it enters between the seatpost and the seat tube. Wait 2–3 minutes and try again. Pull the seatpost all the way out.

INSTALLATION PROCEDURE:

Do this after the seat has been installed on the new seatpost.

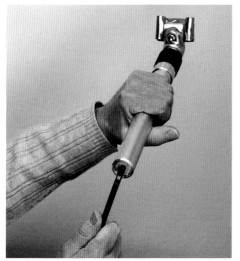

14

Left: Fig. 14.7. Adjusting the tension of a suspension seatpost, or "shockpost." This device is a cheap way to get some cushioning on a hardtail bike.

Above: Fig. 14.8. The internal parts of a suspension seatpost.

1. Apply grease to the inside of the seat tube and the outside of the seatpost.

2. Insert the seatpost in the seat tube.

3. Move it to the exact location where you want it to be, but make sure the marker that shows the minimum insertion depth is not exposed.

4. Holding the seat at the right height and straight ahead, tighten the binder bolt or the quick-release. (If the quick-release can't be tightened properly, flip it to "open" again, adjust the thumb nut on the other side, and try again.)

5. Check to make sure the position is correct, and fine-tune the various adjustments if necessary. You may find that you now need to adjust the angle and forward position in accordance with the applicable instructions above.

NOTE:

• At least 2½ inches (6.5 cm) of the seatpost must be clamped in. Usually the seatpost is marked to show this safe insertion depth.

SUSPENSION SEATPOSTS

These items are surprisingly effective in helping to smooth the ride on "hardtail" bikes, i.e., those without "real" rear suspension. However, a word of warning is in place here: never use a suspension seatpost on a bike with rear suspension, because the effect of the two suspension methods against each other may ruin the more sophisticated rear suspension element.

Preload is the only factor that can be adjusted on the suspension seatpost. To do that, remove the seatpost from the bike, and use an Allen wrench to tighten or loosen the adjuster plug in the bottom of the seatpost. Turning it in tightens the initial compression of the spring element inside; turning it out slackens it. Don't unscrew it so far that any part of the adjuster plug extends from the seatpost end (at least the beginning of the internal screw threads in the seatpost must be visible).

14

Fig. 16.9. Adjusting tension of leather seat cover.

MAINTENANCE OF LEATHER SEAT

A real leather seat stretches with use, especially if it is allowed to get wet. The best way to maintain its integrity is to treat the cover with leather grease (available from the seat manufacturer, but any mineral oil or grease will do in a pinch; just don't use vegetable oil) once or twice a year. Let it sit overnight so it penetrates properly before using the seat. Occasionally, you may also have to tension the seat cover to account for stretch.

TOOLS AND EQUIPMENT:

• special seat wrench available from the seat manufacturer (i.e., probably Brooks, the major surviving leather seat manufacturer)

PROCEDURE:

1. Look under the seat cover near the tip (referred to as the "nose" of the seat) and identify the bolt that holds the tip of the seat cover to the wires, then find the nut on this bolt for adjusting.

2. Tighten the nut by about ½ turn at a time until the seat cover has the right tension. Do not overtighten.

NOTE:

• If the seat cover "sags," flaring out at the sides near the front, you can usually rescue it as follows:

1. Drill a series of four or five $3/32$-inch (2 mm) diameter holes about ¾ inch (20 mm) apart, about ½ inch (12 mm) above the lower edge on both sides of the flared-out area.

2. Using a thin round shoe lace, tie the two sides together into an acceptable shape and tie the ends of the shoe lace together in a firm knot kept out of sight.

14

Fig. 14.10. "Rescuing" a flared-out leather seat cover by lacing it up.

15
FRAME MAINTENANCE

Although the frame is the biggest of the bicycle's components, it's not really subject to the kind of damage that calls for repair and maintenance very much. The few things that can happen—and the even fewer things that can be done about them—are covered in this chapter.

The frame traditionally consists of steel tubing brazed or welded together into a roughly diamond-shaped structure. The frame itself comprises the main frame, built up from large diameter tubing, and the rear triangle made of smaller diameter tubing. The front fork is free to rotate in the main frame's head tube by means of the headset (see Chapter 13).

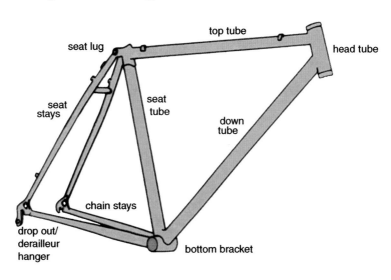

Fig. 15.1. The parts of a typical hardtail mountain bike frame.

In recent years, frame construction and design have changed quite a bit, especially due to the use of different materials and the proliferation of suspension systems. As for materials, most frames are now made of aluminum alloys, while also titanium, carbon fiber, and magnesium are in use.

The problem with all those "new" materials is that frames and forks made with them are even less repairable than steel frames are. The kind of damage that a frame or a fork is likely to sustain is either so minor that it doesn't really matter much (e.g., scratched paint) or so major that it can't be fixed, and requires replacement. Therefore this chapter mainly deals with checking for damage,

rather than actually fixing things once they are damaged. The one thing you can do—at least on a frame made of steel or welded aluminum—is to touch up the paint, and that will be covered at the end of the chapter.

FRAME INSPECTION

After the bike has been in a fall or collision, check it over thoroughly. If there are signs of bending, buckling, or cracking, take it to a bike shop and ask what you should do.

The two most significant areas to watch out for are the front fork and the area of the down tube just behind the lower headset. If you see any bulging or cracking, check with the bike shop (whose advice is probably to discard the frame or the fork). If there is no obvious damage, check for distortion of frame and fork, as per the following procedures.

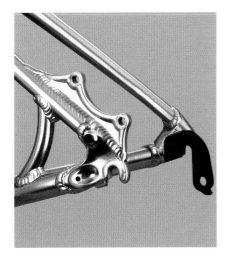

Fig. 15.2. Three modern mountain bike frame details in one picture: Typical separate derailleur hanger dropout (black) on aluminum frame and rear stay bracing (between the left seat-and chain-stays) to provide the stiffness required for use of a rear disk brake, and mounting pad for disk brake caliper unit.

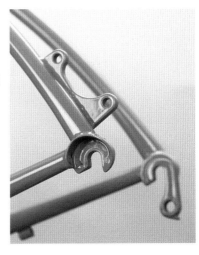

Right: Fig. 15.3. The same detail on a (rare) steel frame. Steel frames are not necessarily heavier, and generally more durable.

FRAME ALIGNMENT CHECK

It's not safe to ride a bike with a frame that is misaligned, meaning that the front and rear wheels don't exactly follow one another in the same track. It negatively affects the balance of the bike, both when going straight and, even more unpredictably, when cornering. You can check the alignment of the frame yourself.

TOOLS AND EQUIPMENT:

- 10 feet (3 m) of twine
- calipers (or straightedge with mm markings)

PROCEDURE:

1. Wrap the twine around the frame from the right-hand rear dropout to the head tube, pull it around and run it back to the left-hand dropout.

2. Measure the distance between the twine and the frame's seat tube on the right and the left and record the results.

3. If the two measurements differ, the frame is misaligned—just how much is too much is up for debate, but I would say that any difference in excess of 3 mm (⅛ inch) is probably unsafe. At least take the bike to a bike shop and ask for advice.

DROPOUT ALIGNMENT CHECK

The dropouts (i.e., the flat plates on which the rear wheel is installed) should be parallel for the wheel to align properly.

TOOLS AND EQUIPMENT:

- 18-inch (45 cm) metal straightedge
- calipers

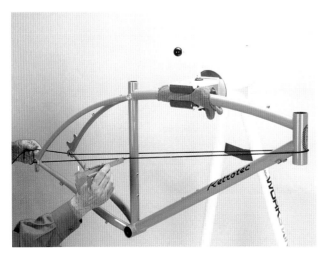

Left and above: Figs. 15.4 and 15.5. Frame alignment check overview (left) and measuring detail at seat tube (above).

PROCEDURE

1. Hold the metal straightedge perpendicular to one of the dropouts, extending in the direction of the seat tube and measure the distance between ruler and seat tube.

2. Do the same on the other dropout.

3. Compare the measurements. Again, there is some latitude for interpretation as to what constitutes unsafe misalignment, but I'd ask for professional advice at a bike shop if the difference is more than 3 mm (1/8 inch).

PAINT TOUCH-UP

When a regular painted, brazed or welded metal frame or fork shows any scratches, you can touch up the paint to prevent rust and to keep the bike looking as nice as possible. Don't do this on carbon-fiber frames, nor on a frame with bonded joints (as opposed to a frame with brazed or welded joints), because the solvents used either in preparation or actual painting may weaken the epoxy, which may void the warranty.

TOOLS AND EQUIPMENT:

• matching paint (if not available from the manufacturer, buy a close match in a model shop or an auto supply store)
• tiny brush
• steel wool or emery cloth
• paint thinner
• cloths

PROCEDURE:

1. Thoroughly clean the area of (and around) the damage.

2. Use emery cloth or a tiny speck of steel wool to remove corrosion, dirt, and paint remnants down to the

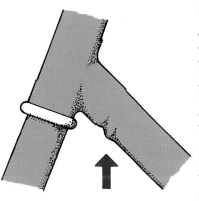

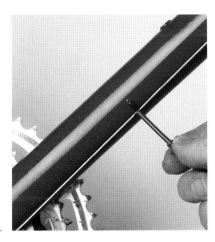

Left: Fig. 15.6. After a frontal crash, check this location for this kind of "buckling" damage to the frame.

Right: Fig. 15.7. Touching up the frame paint.

15

bare, shiny metal surface in the damaged spot.

3. Clean the spot to be repainted once more with a cloth soaked in paint thinner, and wipe it dry.

4. Shake the paint thoroughly to mix it.

5. Using the tiny brush, just barely dipped in paint, apply paint only to the damaged area.

6. Let it dry for at least 24 hours, and repeat steps 4 and 5 if necessary.

REPAINTING A FRAME

It's a major job, and hard to do just right. Don't try to do this on a composite bike, because it will void the warranty (and worse, it may damage the bonding materials used). On a conventional frame, it can be done, and here is how to go about it. Use automotive spray can paint.

15

Before you start, read the instructions on the can and follow them to the letter. But before you make a mess of the frame, waste a can full by practicing on some old pieces of metal. The trick is to pass the spray in a constant, overlapping pattern, starting before you reach the item to be painted, and finishing each pass beyond it.

TOOLS AND EQUIPMENT:

- automotive spray paint (primer and finish coat, available at auto supply stores)
- steel wool or emery cloth
- paint thinner
- cloths
- large dropcloth or cardboard to catch overspray and drips

PREPARATION PROCEDURE:

1. Remove everything from the bike (except perhaps the bottom bracket and the headset cups, providing you cover them well with masking tape.

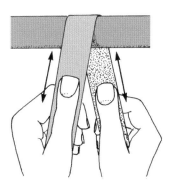
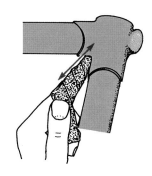

Left: Fig. 15.8. Sanding around the frame tubes.

Right: Fig. 15.9. Sanding in tight corners of the frame.

2. Place plugs (e.g., corks or rolled-up paper) in the places where you don't want paint to enter, such as the seat lug, bottom bracket, and the head tube. Then clean the bike thoroughly.

3. Using either paint stripper or abrasive cloth, remove all traces of the old paint and any traces of rust. Then clean with paint thinner and allow to dry.

4. Hang the item to be painted as shown in Fig. 15.10 in a clean dust-free area, preferably a sheltered outside location.

PAINTING PROCEDURE:

1. Apply what you've learned practicing on the frame and/or the fork, working around systematically, covering all sides and angles equally thoroughly. Use a spoke, hooked in e.g., at a dropout eyelet to turn the frame or the fork.

FINISHING PROCEDURE:

1. Wait at least 24 hours, then check whether the paint is really "cured" (dry and hard) in an unobtrusive place.

2. Once the paint is cured, wait another 24 hours and then use rubbing compound or paint polish to polish out the paint to an even shine.

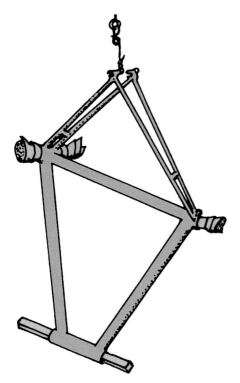

15

Left: Fig. 15.10. Hanging up the frame for painting and drying.

Above: Fig. 15.11. Detail view from below: down tube at head tube joint, showing reinforcing gusset and cable lugs.

16
Front Suspension Maintenance

These days, almost all mountain bikes have at least a front suspension fork. This chapter deals with the front suspension fork, whereas Chapter 17 covers the rear suspension.

Fig. 16.1. Front end of typical modern mountain bike with front suspension.

Suspension Terminology

What's commonly referred to as suspension really comprises two different but related concepts: suspension and damping. Think of the former as "springiness" and the latter as a way of reducing "bounciness" after the suspension's first response to an impact.

If the fork responds immediately to the slightest bump and tends to spring right up again, it has inadequate damping. If it does not respond enough to an impact, it either has too much damping or the spring is too tough for the rider's weight. If it "bottoms out" even in response to moderate bumps, the spring element is too weak for the rider's weight.

The most important measure of suspension is called travel—the difference between the compressed and uncompressed state. You want more for downhill racing in rough terrain than for more modest use.

Two other concepts are preload and "stiction." Preload refers to the amount by which the spring element is compressed even before hitting a bump. Stiction is the initial resistance against movement. For rough terrain, you want more stiction than for a bike ridden mainly on relatively smooth paths.

Preload should be no more than 25 percent of total travel.

SUSPENSION STEMS

This is the simplest, and surprisingly effective way of adding front suspension. You can replace a normal rigid stem by one of these, following the procedure outlined in Chapter 13. You can adjust its spring rate by tightening or loosening an Allen bolt to prestress the spring element.

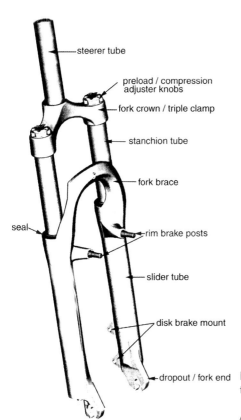

- steerer tube
- preload / compression adjuster knobs
- fork crown / triple clamp
- stanchion tube
- fork brace
- seal
- rim brake posts
- slider tube
- disk brake mount
- dropout / fork end

16

Left: Fig. 16.2. Front suspension fork terminology.

Above: Fig. 16.3. Cleaning the slider tube of a suspension fork.

SUSPENSION FORKS

The most common front suspension is by means of a telescoping suspension fork. These incorporate two sets of tubes that slide inside each other, the inner ones (the stanchion tubes) being guided in the outer ones (called slider tubes) and connected with spring elements. The spring elements are either elastomer pads, metal coil springs, or air cartridges; and different types may be combined on different sides of the same fork. See Fig. 16.2 for the names of the parts of a suspension fork.

By way of preventive maintenance, the most important thing is to keep the seals and the stanchion tubes clean. Do this once a week and after every ride in wet weather or dusty terrain. Wipe the exposed parts of the stanchions and the seals; then apply synthetic oil to these parts and push the fork in five times; then wipe the stanchion tubes off once more.

In addition, check the suspension fork at least once a season to make sure it is working properly, as described below.

SUSPENSION FORK CHECK

TOOLS AND EQUIPMENT:

• Usually none required

PROCEDURE:

1. Holding the bike firmly at the headset, try to wiggle the bottom of the fork at the fork-ends. If they move loosely, you have a problem, which you should refer to a bike shop mechanic.

2. Holding the bike from the front at the handlebars, push down with all your body weight and observe how the suspension fork reacts. If all is

Left: Fig. 16.4. Damping control adjustment.

Right: Fig. 16.5. Compression control adjustment.

well, it goes down with increasing resistance but does not stop suddenly.

3. With the suspension fork pushed in
as in step 2, release pressure and observe whether the recovery is smooth
and quick.

4. If any of the criteria above are not
met, you may have a problem, and
it's recommended you refer it to a
bike shop.

SUSPENSION FORK MAINTENANCE

For this work, refer to the instruction
manual that came with the specific fork.
In addition to cleaning, you may be able
to adjust one or more of the following:

- preload, which controls the response
rate, i.e., how easy it is to compress
the fork
- damping, i.e., how much it see-saws
up and down after compression and
release
- travel, i.e., how far the fork can go
down and back up again (this can
only be adjusted by opening the fork
and replacing its internal parts, and
only on certain models)
- rebound rate, i.e., how quickly it
recovers after compression

On different forks, there may be different methods and locations for making
these adjustments, mainly depending on
the type of spring elements used.

TRAVEL AND PRELOAD CHECK

The manufacturer's fact sheet (provided
with the fork or available on the Web)
states the maximum amount of travel a
fork has. To get the maximum benefit

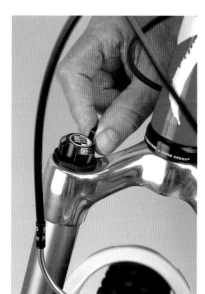

Left: Fig. 16.6.
This fork has a
lever that
allows locking
out the
suspension
fork's re-
sponse.

Right:
Fig. 16.7.
Rebound ad-
justment.

16

from that fork, you need to set it up so that you actually use as much of that available travel as possible. To do that, first measure what I call the "active travel," i.e., the amount of compression you achieve under normal riding conditions.

TOOLS AND EQUIPMENT:

- zip-tie
- calipers

PROCEDURE:

1. Strap the zip-tie tightly around the stanchion tube and push it up against the top of the slider tube.

Fig. 16.8. Measuring the amount of fork travel.

2. Sit on the bike, distributing your weight the same way as you would riding it. This is the passive load and the zip-tie will be pushed down some distance.

3. Get off again and measure the distance between the zip-tie and the top of the slider tube. This distance should be no more than 25 percent of the total available travel (for example, it should not be more than 15 mm on a fork with 60 mm of nominal travel).

4. Go for a 30-minute ride in the most demanding terrain you would typically ride. This zip tie gets pushed up further, and the distance between it and the top of the slider is your active travel. It should be close to the maximum quoted. In fact, it's about right if just once on your ride, you feel the fork bottoming out.

ACTIVE TRAVEL AND PRELOAD ADJUSTMENT

Referring to the information supplied with the fork in question, locate the preload adjuster (usually on top of each stanchion). Turn it to reduce the preload to the lowest value. Then check the ride to see whether it bottoms out on rebound. If it does, adjust the preload up a little. This will give you the maximum amount of effective travel.

16

17
REAR SUSPENSION MAINTENANCE

A s with front suspension, there are a number of different ways to "soften up" the rear end of the bike. As with front suspension, the purpose is not just more comfort but also traction—assuring contact of the wheel with the ground. This chapter deals with the most general issues of rear suspension maintenance.

For the common terminology and general concepts that are common to all forms of suspension, please refer to Chapter 16, where they were described in conjunction with front suspension technology. Unfortunately, the more so-

Figs. 17.1, 17.2, and 17.3. Three different rear suspension designs. Although there are several other methods as well, these three designs are pretty well established.

phisticated, the more troublesome the rear suspension is likely to be. The most sophisticated ones, such as those used on downhill mountain bikes, tend to have many linkages and pivot points, which all add up to potential loose connections, due to wear.

From a maintenance standpoint, there are two important things to watch, and they're common on all those different types: the shock unit, suspension element, itself and the pivot points where the different linkage elements rotate relative to the frame and/or relative to each other.

If you don't want to get more involved, as described below, at least keep all these parts clean, and lightly lubricate the pivot points regularly, using a nongreasy lubricant, such as a wax-based one, or even WD-40. Wipe off any excess lubricant. Also tighten the pivot bolts once a month.

SHOCK UNIT MAINTENANCE

The heart of any rear suspension system is a shock unit, comprising the spring element and a damping device. The spring element may be an external coil spring or a discretely hidden air cartridge. The damping device is usually in the form of an oil cylinder with a piston with valves through which the oil flows as the piston is displaced.

In addition to regularly cleaning the shock unit once a month and after each ride in wet or dusty terrain, inspect the unit once a month. If there are any traces of oil, it means the unit leaks, and it must be replaced.

Replacing the unit involves the same work as described below for a seasonal inspection. Remove the rear wheel before starting this work.

17

Above: Fig. 17.4. Close-up of shock unit and pivots on a multi-pivot system.

Right: Fig. 17.5. Adjusting the rear shock unit's preload.

TOOLS AND EQUIPMENT:

- Allen wrench to fit pivot bolt
- open-ended wrench to fit pivot nut
- cleaning cloths

PROCEDURE:

1. At the front end of the shock unit (where it is attached to the main frame), unscrew the pivot bolt, while holding the nut at the other end.

2. Also undo the pivot bolt in the back (where the unit is attached to the rear triangle).

3. Check the rear triangle (which is now free to move) for any looseness or rough rotation of the pivots. If so, disassemble, clean, lubricate, and/or replace pivot bushings or bearings.

4. Clean and lightly oil exposed parts of the shock unit. Replace if defective.

5. If it's an air-sprung unit that's been losing air pressure, replace the air valve (usually a standard bicycle valve), and reinflate to the specified pressure.

6. Reassemble in reverse sequence. Replace the locking-insert nuts used on the shock unit mounting bolts by new ones.

SUSPENSION TROUBLESHOOTING

Here's a short list of the most common suspension problems and their solution. These points apply both to front and rear suspension.

Left: Fig. 17.6. Removing the shock unit on a single-pivot type rear swing arm.

Right: Fig. 17.7. Lubricating pivot bushings.

17

Problem: Suspension dips even on minor bumps and often bottoms out.

- Cause/Solution: The spring is too weak. If air-sprung, increase air pressure. Otherwise, replace the coil spring or the elastomer pads by higher rated ones.

Problem: Suspension not responsive enough.

- Cause/Solution: The spring is too stiff. If air-sprung, reduce air pressure. Otherwise, replace spring element by a lower rated one.

Problem: Suspension sags more and more as the ride progresses.

- Cause/Solution: Insufficient recovery, or rebound. Adjust the rebound adjuster until the bike absorbs fast, repetitive impacts without loss of stability.

Problem: Suspension stiffens up progressively as the ride progresses.

- Cause/Solution: Too much compression stage damping. Adjust for less compression stage damping.

Problem: Unequal responsiveness between front and rear suspension.

- Cause/Solution: Non-compatible spring elements front and rear. Choose fork and rear shock with similar amounts of travel. Whereas it's fixed in the rear, you may be able to replace the front fork elements by ones with more (or less) travel.

Problem: Unpredictable behavior of rear end of the bike while turning.

- Cause/Solution: Remove the shock unit and check for resistance. If it feels too soft, have it overhauled or replaced.

Fig. 17.8. Checking pivot bolts. These bolts must also be removed to clean and lubricate the pivot bushings.

17

18 ACCESSORY MAINTENANCE

An accessory, as opposed to a component, is defined as any part that is, or can be, installed on the bike but is not part of its essential operation. In this chapter, we'll deal with the most common accessories for use with the mountain bike.

Thousands of accessories have been introduced for bicycle use at different times, and hundreds are available today. What they all have in common is some kind of attachment to the bike. And that's indeed the most common maintenance aspect of all components. In addition, there will be some more specific advice concerning the most important and/ or common accessories in use today:

- lights
- reflectors
- pump
- lock
- bicycle computer
- luggage racks
- fenders

Fig. 18.1. An older mountain bike with a pretty full complement of accessories.

GENERAL ACCESSORY COMMENTS

The two rules of accessory maintenance are:
- keep it tightly mounted
- replace (or remove) it if it's broken

The last thing you want on the bike is an accessory that hangs loose or doesn't even do its job. Check the installation hardware regularly, tightening all nuts, bolts, and clamps. And by all means, remove the item if it doesn't work and you haven't been able to fix it. Before replacing it in that case, ask yourself whether you could do without it altogether, and don't replace it unless you have to.

Generally, any attachment hardware should have at least two mounting bolts, so vibration is less likely to rattle it loose. Another thing to watch out for is that items clamped around another part of the bike should fit snugly—and pref-

erably there should be a flexible plastic or rubber protective sleeve around the bicycle component, which helps protect the bike's finish and aids in keeping the accessory mounting hardware in place.

LIGHTING EQUIPMENT MAINTENANCE

Nighttime cycling no longer has to be the dangerous undertaking which it was considered to be some 20 years ago. Today, excellent lighting systems and individual lights—both front and rear—are readily available at most bike shops.

Although generator (dynamo) lights are OK for road use, the only type of lights suitable for off-road use are those using batteries. These fall into two major categories:
- battery lights with built-in batteries in the light unit
- battery lights with separate, central battery.

LIGHTS WITH BUILT-IN BATTERIES

Fig. 18.2. Check the installation of any accessories from time to time, tightening all nuts and bolts.

In the front, these are usually clamped directly or indirectly to the handlebars. In the rear, they are usually attached to the seatpost. The one used for the front should be bright and produce a compact bundle of light illuminating an area about 20–33 feet (6–10 m) in front of the bike. Usually, there's a clamp that stays on the handlebars once installed

18

and the light just slides and clips into this clamp, so you can remove it when you leave the bike unguarded.

The rear light should be red, and point straight back (neither up nor down, neither left nor right). The rear light does not need to be quite so bright as the one in front. LEDs (Light-Emitting Diodes) appear to be very suitable for this use, mainly because they provide much longer battery life. The LEDs themselves also last much longer than light bulbs—however, they don't last forever either, and the light will have to be replaced if they become dim.

The most common maintenance required on battery lights is replacing the batteries and the bulbs. A battery charge typically lasts less than 3 hours, so it's a good idea to carry spares (and especially if you use rechargeable ones, recharge them at least once a month, even if they haven't been used). Before you go on a longer ride that may take you in the evening, check the condition of both the batteries in the light and the spare batteries.

If you use rechargeable batteries, note the difference between the two most common types of lights. If the lights are designed for standard-size cells, both NiCad (Nickel-Cadmium) and NiMH (Nickel-Metal-Hydride) rechargeable batteries are available. NiMH batteries last considerably longer but are more expensive. However, since they also have a longer shelf life (i.e., they will hold a charge when not used much longer), they're worth the extra.

Bulbs typically don't last more than about 100 hours of use. Get some spare bulbs and carry one for each light on the bike, e.g., in the tire patch kit. If you use the nice bright halogen bulbs, don't touch the glass with your bare hands, because the acidity will etch the glass dull, reducing their light output once they get hot.

Lights with LEDs instead of bulbs are very energy-efficient (long battery life) and have a long bulb life. In the past, these were only available in versions

Left: Fig. 18.3. Simple front light with internal batteries.

Right: Fig. 18.4. Battery-operated rear light unit. With its flashing LEDs, the batteries in this kind of light can last a long time.

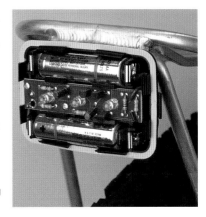

18

that, though quite visible to others, their light output was not enough to use them as headlights. However, modern (and quite expensive) versions with LEDs are much brighter and can be used instead of lights with regular halogen bulbs.

In flashing mode, their batteries last at least 100 hours (less when burning constantly, but still much longer than with standard bulbs) C and they are more visible in flashing mode.

LIGHTS WITH CENTRAL BATTERY

These lights are typically more powerful and often have high beam and low beam capabilities. Their larger battery, consisting of several cells wired up together,

are either packaged in a pouch tied to the bike or neatly packed away in something that fits in a water bottle cage (actually, a real water bottle is often used, with the battery cells inserted and the space around them filled with some kind of compound to keep everything in place).

Again, the batteries and the bulbs need to be checked and replaced if necessary (and if those batteries are rechargeable, just plug the unit in via its adapter, which should recharge them in about 3 hours). In addition to NiCad and NiMH batteries, there are also lead-acid gel batteries. The latter require different care: they have to be recharged *before* they are fully discharged, i.e., before the light gets dim, whereas the

Left: Fig. 18.5. Typical central-battery operated lighting system with batteries sealed in a water bottle.

Above: Fig. 18.6. Modern LED-lights get more light out of a single battery and are probably the wave of the future.

18

other types seem to last longest if they are drained completely before they are recharged. See the preceding section *Battery Lights With Built-In Battery* for more information regarding spare bulbs and batteries.

In addition to bulbs and batteries, there is wiring to deal with. So, if the light doesn't work and you've checked the bulb and the battery, and found them to be OK, check the wiring. Usually it's a connection at the end of the wiring, so check there first and fix it with a soldering iron and solder. If there are any exposed metal wire parts, use electrical insulating tape to fix it. You may have to replace the wiring completely if you can't identify the source of the problem.

REFLECTORS

The law in the U.S. and most other Western countries requires bicycles to be equipped with a number of reflectors when used on the road at night. Don't think they're substitutes for lights: they're only useful in addition to lights, and they're not much help out on the trail, because they rely on the headlights of another vehicle. Just the same, when riding on public roads, the rear reflector makes you quite visible to following cars.

Make sure the reflectors are mounted firmly and point straight back (for the one in the rear) and forward (for the one in the front). Although the

one in the back can give adequate protection against following motorists, never solely rely on the one in front—get a front light instead. Lights are more visible over a wider angle of coverage for all directions from which you may be endangered and they allow you to see where you're going yourself.

Replace any reflector that is cracked or broken, because water can enter through the crack and "fog up" the reflective pattern on the inside of the lens, making it "blind."

PUMP

I suggest you use two kinds of pumps: a floor pump for at home and a frame-mounted hand pump for on the road. Once or twice a year, tighten the screw

Fig. 18.7. This rear reflector is built into the back of the seat.

cap at the head. If the pump doesn't work, first take the head apart. Sometimes you can get by with turning the flexible grommet (that's a thick washer) around, or you may have to replace it.

The other item that sometimes gives trouble is the rubber or plastic plunger inside the barrel. It can be reached by unscrewing the cap at the point where the plunger mechanism enters the barrel. Flex it, knead it, apply some lubricant to it, and if you can't get it to work, you'll probably have to replace the pump unless you can find a replacement.

BICYCLE COMPUTER

Bicycle computers have also improved dramatically over time. Even so, they're still fidgety items. Check the installation of the pickup that's attached to a spoke, and the matching sensor, to make sure they pass each other closely. Check the condition of the wire, and tie it down at intermediate points with zip-ties or electric insulating tape so they don't get

caught or damaged. And again, if it doesn't work, replace or discard the entire system, computer, mounting bracket, sensor, pick-up, wire, and all.

LOCK

There's not much maintenance required on this, unfortunately, most essential accessory. Lubrication is done once or twice a year by inserting the nozzle of a thin lubricant, such as WD-40, at the point where the bolt enters into the lock mechanism and spraying in just a tiny little squirt of oil. In addition, you can put some oil on the key, insert it in the lock, and then close and open the lock 2 or 3 times to lubricate it. If your lock can be attached to the bike frame, check and tighten the bolts of the clamp that holds it during the monthly inspection.

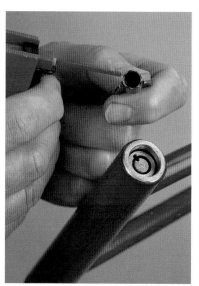

Left: Fig. 18.8. The essential parts of a bicycle pump.

Right: Fig. 18.9. On the lock, lightly lubricate the shackle and the key once or twice a year.

18

Luggage Rack

Luggage racks, or carriers, are available both for the front and the rear. For bikes with front suspension, only the rear-mounted racks are suitable. And if the bike also has rear suspension, the only racks suitable are those that clamp to the seatpost (and won't take a heavy load).

For the installation of racks, it's preferable if the frame and the front fork have brazed-on bosses and eyelets at the dropouts and fork ends to attach the rack to. If there are no bosses and eyelets, you can install clips around seat

stays in the rear of a hardtail bike.

Fenders

Both during and after rainfall, fenders (mud guards) help keep water and mud off the bike, the rider, and those following behind.

Make sure they're firmly connected at the various mounting points. Also check to make sure they don't rub against the tire or another moving part. Check the connections regularly and tighten the hardware—or discard the fender if you can't get it tight enough.

Above: Fig. 18.10. Typical cycle computer installation.

Right: Figs. 18.11 and 18.12. Luggage racks. On a full-suspension bike, use the type that is clamped around the seatpost (lower image).

18

WARNING DEVICES

Either a bell, a horn, or a whistle will alert others to your presence, but only the first will identify you as a cyclist. Besides, out in nature, the blast of a horn, or even the shrieking of a whistle seems more misplaced than the modest but distinctive sound of a bell. Mount it within easy reach, and keep the mounting bolt tight. If there's a metal mechanism inside, give it a drop of oil twice a year.

WATER BOTTLE CAGE

Despite the current popularity of back-pack-carried "hydration systems," the old fashioned bicycle water bottle is still a good standby. Install a water bottle cage on the frame tube bosses provided for that purpose on most frames, using 4 mm Allen bolts and washers.

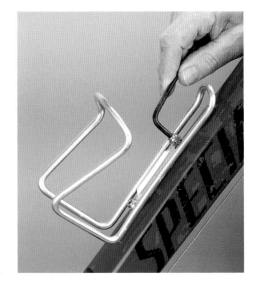

Above: Fig. 18.13. A bell is a rather civilized warning device as compared to yelling or blowing a horn.

Right: Fig. 18.14. Installing water bottle cage.

18

BIBLIOGRAPHY

Barnett, John. *Barnett's Manual: Analysis and Procedures for Bike Mechanics*. 4th. Ed. Boulder, CO: VeloPress, 2001.

Berto, Frank. *The Dancing Chain: History and Development of the Derailleur Bicycle*. San Francisco: Van der Plas Publications, 2005.

—. *Bicycling Magazine's Complete Guide to Upgrading Your Bicycle*. Emmaus, PA: Rodale Press, 1989.

—. *The Birth of Dirt: The Origins of Mountain*. San Francisco: Van der Plas Publications, 1998.

Brandt, Jobst. *The Bicycle Wheel*. 3rd. Ed. Palo Alto: Avocet, 1995.

Break It, Fix It, Ride It. (Compact Disk). Pittsford, NY: Break It, Fix It, Ride It, Inc., 2001.

Burrows, Mike. *Bicycle Design: Towards the Perfect Machine*. York (GB): Open Road / Seattle: Alpenbooks, 2000.

Cole, Clarence, H. J. Glenn, John S. Allen. *Glenn's New Complete Bicycle Manual*. New York: Crown Publishers, 1987.

Cuthberson, Tom. *Anybody's Bike Book*. Berkeley, CA: Ten-Speed Press, 1998.

DeLong, Fred: *DeLong's Guide to Bicycles and Bicycling: The Art and Science*. 2nd Edn. Radnor, PA: Chilton Books, 1978.

Downs, Todd. *The Bicycling Guide to Complete Bicycle Maintenance & Repair*. Emmaus, PA: Rodale Press, 2005.

Jones, Calvin W. *Big Blue Book of Bicycle Repair*. St Paul (MN): Park Tool Co., 2005.

Milson, Fred. *Complete Bike Maintenance*. Osceola, WI: MBI Publishing, 2003.

Oliver, Tony. *Touring Bikes: A Practical Guide*. Ramsbury (GB): Crowood Press, 1990.

Ries, Richard. *Building Your Perfect Bike: From Bare Frame to Personalized Superbike*. Osceola, WI: MBI Publishing, 1997.

Roegner, Thomas. *Mountain Bike Maintenance and Repair*. San Francisco: Van der Plas Publications, 2004.

Sutherland, Howard. *Sutherland's Handbook for Bicycle Mechanics*. 5th Edn. Berkeley, CA: Sutherland Publications, 2006.

Van der Plas, Rob. *The Bicycle Repair Book*. 2nd Edn. San Francisco: Bicycle Books, 1993.

——. *Bicycle Technology: Understanding, Selecting, and Maintaining the Modern Bicycle and its Components*. San Francisco: Bicycle Books, 1991.

——. *Buying a Bike: How to Get the Best Bike for Your Money*. San Francisco: Van der Plas Publications, 1999.

Zinn, Lennard. *Zinn and the Art of Mountain Bike Maintenance*. Boulder, CO: VeloPress, 1995.

——. *Mountain Bike Performance Handbook*. Osceola, WI: MBI Publishing, 1998.

INDEX